Alfred's Self-Teaching Adult Piano Course

The new, easy and fun way to teach yourself to play

WILLARD A. PALMER • MORTON MANUS

Playing the Piano

Playing the piano is more than just pressing down some keys. Sure, it will bring music into your home, but it can do so much more than that. For many of us, listening to or performing music brings joy, pleasure and relaxation into our lives. It can take away, for a short time at least, the cares and tensions of a troubled world.

After a while, you will be able to play for friends and enjoy having them sing along with you. Many adult students quickly progress to the point where they can perform at birthday parties and yes, we have included *Happy Birthday to You* in our book. At Christmas time, you will be able to perform *Joy to the World*, and that is also included. Fairly soon, and sooner than you might think, you will be able to perform at gatherings of all kinds. The more you get involved with music, the more interesting and exciting your life can become.

What makes this course even more special are the unique *Study Guides* that precede every music page. The *Study Guides* offer explanations, directions and additional information to help you more easily understand how to play. It becomes, in fact, your at-home teacher, assuring you of a quicker, more successful and more enjoyable learning experience.

Also invaluable is the enclosed CD that contains a recording of every song title in the book. Listening or playing along with the recording is not only fun to do but helps to reinforce musical concepts such as rhythm, dynamics and phrasing. For convenience, you may download the CD onto an MP3 player, digital music player or iPod® and have it with you as you play the piano.

Morty Manus

ISBN-10: 0-7390-5205-5
ISBN-13: 978-0-7390-5205-1

Contents

2

The Study Guides

The *Study Guides* (usually the left page) always precede the music page (usually the following right page) and offer explanations, directions and additional information to help you learn and perform the music page. It becomes, in fact, your at-home teacher.

If you already have a piano teacher, the *Study Guide* page can still be your teacher between lessons. But if time constraints and scheduling problems make regular lessons difficult, then these teaching pages will help you learn to play on your own. Generally speaking, however, you will progress more easily and quickly with a professional—and remember that you can always begin with a teacher at any time, no matter how far you have progressed in this book.

So let's get started now. There is a lot to do but the important thing is that you are going to have a lot of fun along the way. You will work hard from time to time but you will enjoy it. More importantly, we will be doing it together.

How to Sit at the Piano

Even if you have played the piano before, it might be worth while to quickly read through page 5, *How to Sit at the Piano.* You'll probably want to start playing right away but a few minutes at the beginning will help you play in the proper sitting position. You'll want to feel comfortable when you play, from the top of your head all the way down to your feet. Sitting up straight is a good way to sit even when you're not playing the piano. Read through page 5 while sitting at the piano, follow the instructions, and imagine you are playing the piano.

How to Sit at the Piano

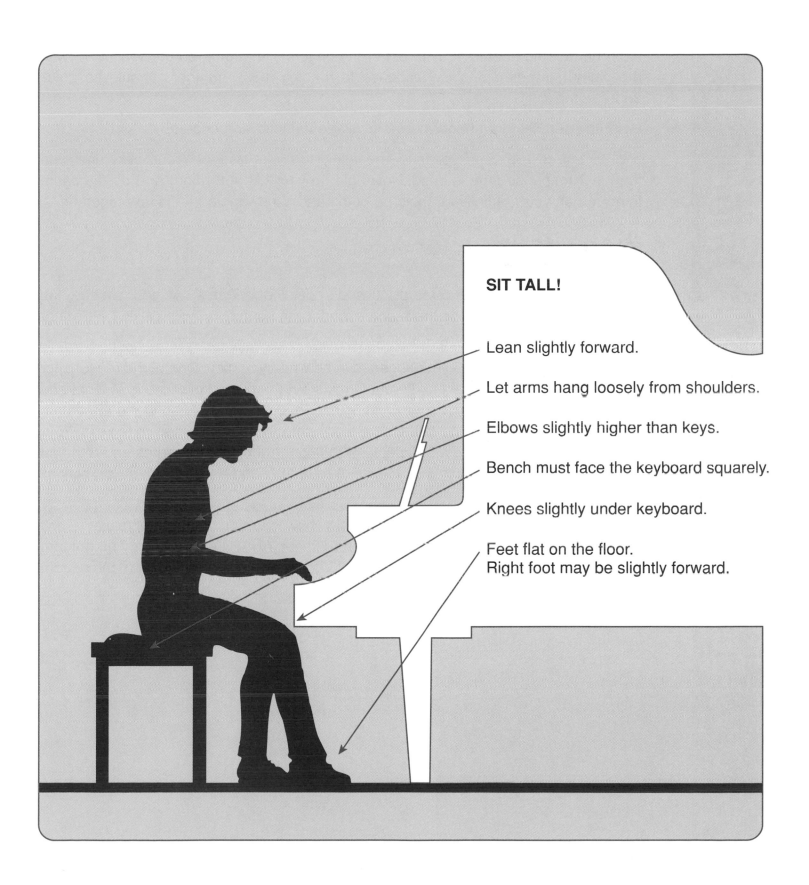

SIT TALL!

Lean slightly forward.

Let arms hang loosely from shoulders.

Elbows slightly higher than keys.

Bench must face the keyboard squarely.

Knees slightly under keyboard.

Feet flat on the floor.
Right foot may be slightly forward.

Finger Numbers

Under the title *Finger Numbers* on page 7, there is a diagram of both hands and how the fingers are numbered. When you begin reading music, there will be numbering suggestions in the music for fingering some of the keys. The thumb of each hand is numbered 1. The rest of the fingers are numbered consecutively, with the pinky numbered 5. Your response to reading these numbers should be quick and automatic.

Hold up your RH (right hand) now and wiggle the following fingers:

3–5–2–1–4–3–1–2–5–4. Continue repeating this exercise on your own until you feel your response time is good. Now hold up your LH (left hand) and do the same thing. When you are finished, hold up both hands and wiggle the fingers together.

Piano Tones

The mechanics of the piano are discussed under *Piano Tones*. As you can see, the harder and faster you press the key, the louder the sound you will make. A little later on, we'll tell you how the piano got its name.

It is very important to keep your fingers curved when you play. One of the reasons for this is that your fingers are of different lengths but the piano keyboard is straight and level. By cupping your hand over an imaginary bubble, all the fingers and the thumb can line up in a straight line that fits perfectly onto five consecutive white keys. Your hand is a truly remarkable instrument—with fingers of different lengths and a thumb that moves more easily from side to side. A rounded hand and 10 fingers can play all 88 keys of the piano keyboard!

Whenever you play, you should always decide how loud or soft you want to play. Don't strike the key too hard or you might hurt your finger. Always be aware of your posture and hand position. Now read through page 7 and play the two exercises at the bottom of the page as directed.

Finger Numbers

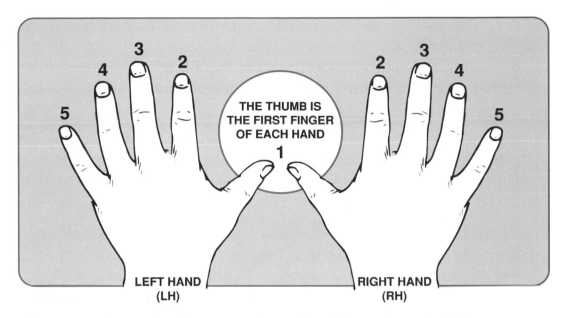

Response to reading finger numbers should be automatic. Before you begin to play, practice moving each finger as you say its number aloud.

Piano Tones

When you play a key, a hammer inside your piano touches a string to make a tone.

When you drop into a key with a LITTLE weight, you make a SOFT tone.

When you use MORE weight, you make a LOUDER tone.

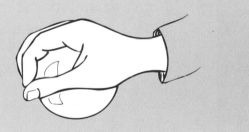

Curve your fingers when you play!

Pretend you have a bubble in your hand.

Hold the bubble gently, so it doesn't break!

1. Play any white key with the 3rd finger of either hand, softly.

2. See how many times you can repeat the same key, making each tone a little louder.

Before you play any key, you should always decide how soft or loud you want it to sound.

For the first pieces in this book, play with a MODERATELY LOUD tone.

The Keyboard

As a teacher, I have often noticed that when adults understand the basics of the instrument and sit properly in front of the piano using good hand positions, they progress more quickly—so a little more time now will produce better results in the long term. For now, let's proceed at a slow but steady rate.

As you sit at the keyboard in a proper playing position, let's get a little more familiar with the piano keyboard. If all the keys were white, it would be very difficult to identify individual keys. Hundreds of years ago, a very wise instrument manufacturer figured out that by producing a keyboard with alternating groups of two and three black keys mixed together with white keys, it would be much easier to quickly identify any key.

Using your 3rd finger of your LH, play any black key on the left side of the keyboard— hear how low the tone sounds? Then, with the 3rd finger of your RH, play any black key on the right side of the keyboard. Hear how much higher the tone sounds? What you have now observed is that as you move to the left on the keyboard, the tones sound *lower*, and as you move to the right on the keyboard, the tones sound *higher*. See how easy this is going to be?

Play the 2-BLACK-KEY groups!

Follow the directions on the lower half of page 9. Using LH fingers 2–3, play any two black keys from the 2-black-key group on the left side of the keyboard, playing both keys at once. Then repeat the same procedure with your RH fingers 2–3, playing any two black keys from the 2-black-key group on the right side of the keyboard, once again playing both keys at once.

Play the 3-BLACK-KEY groups!

Finally, using the same procedure you used for the 2-black-key group, with LH fingers 2–3–4, play any three keys from the 3-black-key group on the left side of the keyboard, playing all three notes at once. Then repeat the same procedure, using RH fingers 2–3–4 on the right side of the keyboard.

You are now ready to read through page 9. Follow the instructions and play exercises 1, 2, 3 and 4 on the bottom half of the page.

The Keyboard

The keyboard is made up of white keys and black keys.

The black keys are in groups of twos and threes.

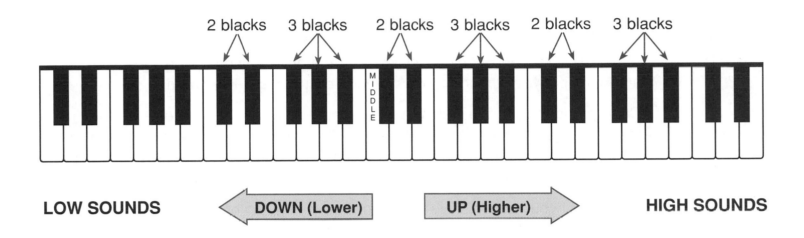

On the keyboard, DOWN is to the LEFT, and UP is to the RIGHT.

As you move LEFT, the tones sound LOWER. As you move RIGHT, the tones sound HIGHER.

Play the 2-BLACK-KEY groups!

LH

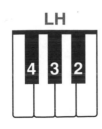

1. Using LH 2 3, begin at the middle and play all the 2-black-key groups going ◁DOWN the keyboard (both keys at once).

2. Using RH 2 3, begin at the middle and play all the 2-black-key groups going UP▷ the keyboard (both keys at once).

RH

Play the 3-BLACK-KEY groups!

LH

3. Using LH 2 3 4, begin at the middle and play all the 3-black-key groups going ◁DOWN the keyboard (all three keys at once).

4. Using RH 2 3 4, begin at the middle and play all the 3-black-key groups going UP▷ the keyboard (all three keys at once).

RH

Name That Key!

A full sized piano keyboard is made up of 88 keys—36 black ones and 52 white. By becoming familiar with the alternating 2- and 3-black-key groups, you will now be able to easily identify any white key on the keyboard. As you probably know, each piano key is given a letter name but only the first 7 letters of the alphabet are used: A–B–C–D–E–F and G.

Here is the secret to easily naming all of the 52 white keys on the keyboard: each white key is recognized by its relationship to a black key group! For example, all A's are found between the top 2 black keys of each 3-black-key group.

Once you identify A, the rest is easy. The letter name of each white key to the right is the next letter of the alphabet: B–C–D–E–F–G. And what happens when you get to G? You're correct if you said we start all over again beginning with A. This higher A is still located between the top two black keys of the 3-black-key group.

I would like you now to follow the instructions on the top of page 11 and play and say the name of each white key, one after the other, until you reach G. After completing this exercise, follow the instructions below the keyboard on the bottom of the page for another exercise.

Middle C

Take particular notice of *Middle C*. It is a very important key and it is located in the middle of the keyboard. Starting all the way to the left of the keyboard on A and using LH 3, play every white key one after the other, saying the letter name as you play. When you get to *Middle C*, switch hands and using RH 3, continue up the keyboard until you reach the highest key, C. After completing this exercise, you will then have played every white key on the keyboard.

I want you to work on your own now, starting at the top of page 11 and follow the directions. Take your time playing and saying all the key names. When you reach the bottom of the page and you feel you can randomly select any key on the keyboard and name it quickly, you will know the names of all the white keys.

Name That Key!

Piano keys are named for the first seven letters of the alphabet, beginning with **A**.

A B C D E F G

Each white key is recognized by its position in or next to a black-key group!

For example: **A**'s are found between the **TOP TWO KEYS** of each **3-BLACK-KEY GROUP**.

Play the following. Use LH 3 for keys below the middle of the keyboard.
Use RH 3 for keys above the middle of the keyboard.

Say the name of each key aloud as you play!

Play all the **A**'s
on your piano.

Play all the **B**'s.

Play all the **C**'s.

Play all the **D**'s.

Play all the **E**'s.

Play all the **F**'s.

Play all the **G**'s.

You can now name every white key on your piano!

The key names are **A B C D E F G**, used over and over!

The lowest key
on your piano
is **A**.

The C nearest the
middle of the piano
is called **MIDDLE C.**

The highest key
on your piano
is **C**.

Going **UP** the keyboard, the notes sound **HIGHER and HIGHER!**

Play and name every white key beginning with bottom A.

Use LH 3 for keys below middle C, and RH 3 for keys above middle C.

Right Hand C Position

Now that you know how to sit at the piano, know how to curve your fingers, and know the numbers of each finger and the names of the keys, we're almost ready to begin playing.

Looking at the keyboard diagram under *Right Hand C Position* on page 13, place your RH on your piano keyboard with your thumb or 1st finger on middle C, your 2nd finger on D, 3rd on E, 4th on F, and 5th on G. After positioning your hand on the keyboard, play keys C-D-E-F-G in that order going to the right, one at a time while saying the finger numbers first, then repeat saying the note names. Now play G-F-E-D-C in that order going to the left, also saying the finger numbers first; then repeat, saying the note names. Notice the sound of the keys go higher as you go to the right, and lower as you go to the left.

The Treble Staff

Just as the letters of the alphabet are used to form written words that allow writers to communicate their *ideas* to you, notes written on a music staff of 5 lines and 4 spaces allow a composer to communicate their *musical ideas* to you.

Look at the lower keyboard diagram on the right side of page 13. Just above it is a music staff, made up of 5 lines and 4 spaces, on which notes are written. On the left side of the staff, and just under the word *fingering*, is a symbol called the **treble clef**. This symbol identifies the specific portion of the keyboard that sounds *higher* and is usually, but not always, played by the RH. A staff beginning with this symbol is called the **treble staff**. Additional short lines, called **leger lines**, sometimes called **ledger lines**, can be added below or above the staff to extend the range of the written notes on the keyboard.

Look at the first note after the treble clef sign—that is middle C and it is written *on* the ledger line just below the staff. D, the next note to the right, is written *in* the space just below the staff. Counting up on the staff, the next note E is written *on* the first line, F is written *in* the first space, and G is written *on* the second line.

RIGHT HAND WARM-UP

Read through the instructions under *Right Hand Warm-Up* and play each line of music twice—say the finger numbers the first time, but thereafter, say only the note names. Start slowly and gradually increase your speed but don't go too fast. For now, the letter name will be written within the note to allow you to become familiar with its location on the staff. We will gradually reduce this lettering so you should try to become familiar with the location of each note of the staff. Starting at the top of page 13, read the instructions and play the exercises on the piano.

Right Hand C Position

Place the RH on the keyboard so that the **1st FINGER** falls on **MIDDLE C.**
Let the remaining 4 fingers fall naturally on the next 4 white keys.
Keep the fingers curved and relaxed.

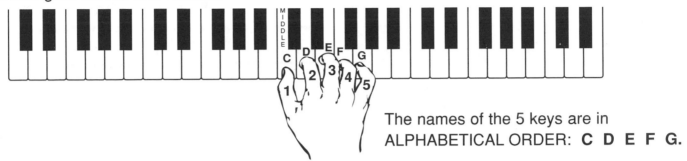

The names of the 5 keys are in
ALPHABETICAL ORDER: **C D E F G.**

Notes for this position are written on the TREBLE STAFF.

The TREBLE STAFF has 5 lines and 4 spaces.

Middle C is written on a short line
below the staff, called a *leger* line.

D is written in the space below the staff.

Each next higher note is written
on the next higher line or space.

TREBLE CLEF SIGN:
used for RH notes.

Fingering:

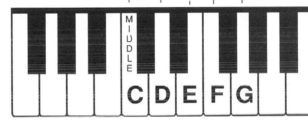

RIGHT HAND WARM-UP

Play the following *WARM-UP.* Say the name of each note aloud as you play.
Repeat until you can play smoothly and evenly. As the notes go higher on the keyboard,
they are written higher on the staff!

Quarter Notes & Half Notes

While you continue to work on controlling your fingers to play evenly, you are going to learn how to play and combine both short tones and long tones. Short and long tones are written as *notes* and we measure their lengths by **counting**. For music to have style, appeal and variety, it requires notes of different lengths combined in uniquely creative patterns. This is called *rhythm.*

Look at the large pink boxes on page 15. The one on the left contains a **quarter note**—the note you played in RH Warm-Up on page 13. It is a short note, and it receives **one count: 1**.

The large box on the right contains a **half note**. It is a longer note and it receives **two counts: 1–2**.

Below the two boxes is a row of notes. Notice that the notes are divided by small, vertical lines, called **bar lines**. The notes *between* the bar lines are called **measures**, and they make up small sections of a larger piece. Measures can also be called **bars**, and that is why bars that divide the measures are called **bar lines**. Each measure usually has the exact same duration as every other measure in a piece.

Music is read from left to right, so beginning all the way to the left on this first line, clap and count each note slowly and evenly. Count measure 1 like this: 1, 1, 1, 1. Count measure 2: 1, 1, 1–2. Count measure 3: 1, 1, 1, 1. And finally, count measure 4: 1–2, 1-2.

On the extreme right of the first line, there is a **double bar line**, and that usually indicates the end of a piece. As you probably noticed, each measure has 4 beats. As the half note receives 2 beats (or half of the 4 beats in a measure), you can see why it is called a **half note.** Similarly, the quarter note receives 1 beat (or one-quarter of the 4 beats) and so it is called a **quarter note.**

ODE TO JOY

You are now ready to play your first musical piece. It is called *Ode to Joy* and was written by Ludwig van Beethoven, a very famous classical composer who lived in the 1800s. *Ode to Joy* also happens to be the official anthem of the European Union.

I would like you to go through the 4 practice steps under the title by yourself. Repeat each step several times until you feel comfortable with it. Play with a moderate tone, not too soft or too loud. When you can play *Ode to Joy* slowly and steadily, you will be ready for the next page.

Quarter Notes & Half Notes

Music is made up of **short** tones and **long** tones. We write these tones in **notes,** and we measure their lengths by **counting**. The combining of notes into patterns is called RHYTHM.

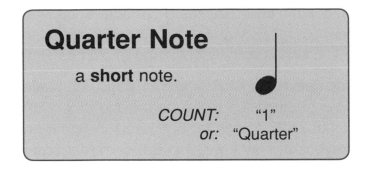

Quarter Note

a **short** note.

COUNT: "1"
or: "Quarter"

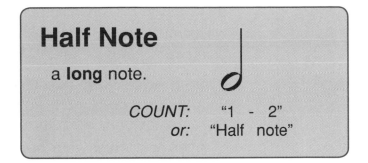

Half Note

a **long** note.

COUNT: "1 - 2"
or: "Half note"

Clap (or tap) the following rhythm. Clap ONCE for each note, counting aloud.

Notice how the BAR LINES divide the music into MEASURES of equal duration.

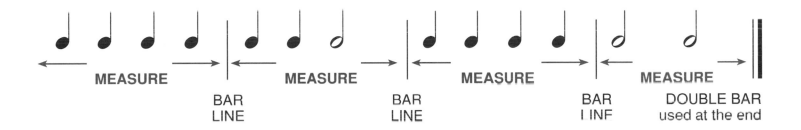

←———— MEASURE ————→ | ←———— MEASURE ————→ | ←———— MEASURE ————→ | ←———— MEASURE ————→

BAR LINE   BAR LINE   BAR LINE   DOUBLE BAR used at the end

ODE TO JOY *(Theme from Beethoven's 9th Symphony)* 🔊

1. Clap (or tap) the rhythm evenly, counting aloud.

2. Play & sing (or say) the finger numbers.

3. Play & count.

4. Play & sing (or say) the note names.

Fingers:

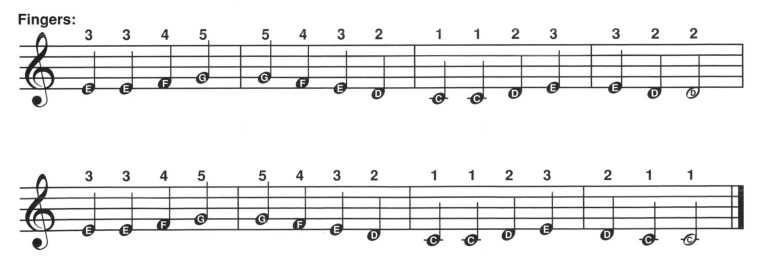

* 🔊 This symbol indicates the track number of the music on the enclosed CD.

Left Hand C Position

The piano has a wide range of tones, from very low on the left side of the keyboard to very high on the right. The LH usually plays the lower tones and the RH usually plays the higher tones. You've just learned to play C to G with the RH and now we will begin playing with the left, also playing C to G, but in a lower keyboard position. Soon, you will combine both hands within one piece, but for now and until you get comfortable using each hand separately, you will play music using only one hand at a time.

Looking at the keyboard diagram under *Left Hand C Position* on page 17, place your LH on your piano keyboard with your 5th finger on the C **below** and to the **left** of middle C, your 4th finger on D, 3rd finger on E, 2nd finger on F, and 1st finger on G. After positioning your hand on the keyboard, play keys C-D-E-F-G in that order and one at a time while saying the finger numbers first. Then repeat saying the note names. Now play G-F-E-D-C in that order, also saying the finger numbers first; then repeat, saying the note names. Notice the sound of the keys go higher as you go to the right, and lower as you go to the left.

Bass Clef

Look at the lower keyboard diagram on the right side of page 17. Just above it is another music staff, but this time on the left and under the word *fingering*, there is a symbol called the **bass clef**. This symbol, similar to the treble clef, identifies a specific portion of the keyboard that sounds *lower* and is usually, but not always, played by the LH. A staff beginning with this symbol is called the **bass staff**.

The bass staff also has 5 lines and 4 spaces but this time, and counting *up*, the first note after the bass clef sign is C written *in* the second space. The next note D is written *on* the third line, E is written *in* the third space, F is written *on* the fourth line, and G is written *in* the fourth space.

LEFT HAND WARM-UP

Read through the instructions under *Left Hand Warm-Up* and play each line of music, saying each note name as you play. Start slowly and gradually increase your speed but, as with your RH, don't go too fast. Play each line twice—say the finger numbers the first time, but thereafter, say only the note names.

Left Hand C Position

Place the LH on the keyboard so that the **5th FINGER** falls on the **C BELOW** (to the left of) **MIDDLE C.**
Let the remaining fingers fall naturally on the next 4 white keys.
Keep the fingers curved and relaxed.

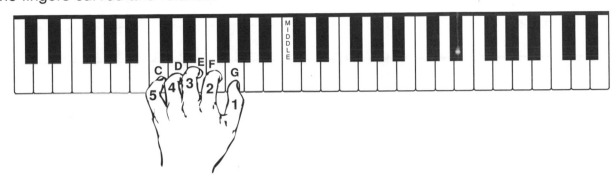

Notes for this position are written on the BASS STAFF.

The BASS STAFF also has
5 lines and 4 spaces.

The C, played by 5,
is written on the
second space of the staff.

Each next higher note is written
on the next higher line or space.

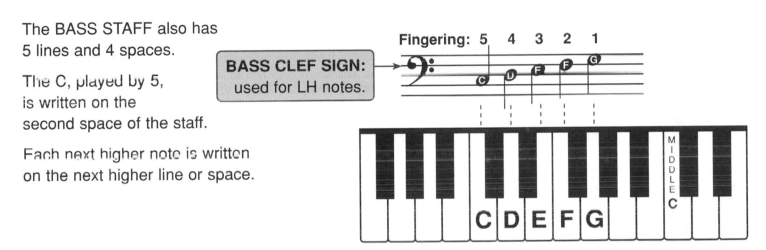

LEFT HAND WARM-UP

Play the following *WARM-UP.* Say the name of each note aloud as you play.
Repeat until you can play smoothly and evenly.

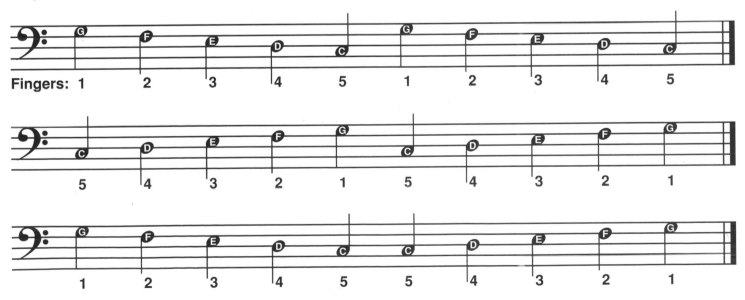

When notes are BELOW the MIDDLE LINE of the staff, the stems usually point UP.
When notes are ON or ABOVE the MIDDLE LINE, the stems usually point DOWN.

The Whole Note

So far, you have learned about **quarter notes**, which receive one count, and **half notes**, which receive two counts. Now you will learn about a new note, a **whole note**. The large box at the top of page 19 shows you what the note looks like. It is basically an oval in shape, almost round.

The whole note is a very long note—and it receives **four counts**. As you already know, in a measure of four counts, the quarter note receives one-quarter of the counts (or 1), and the half note receives one-half of the counts (or 2). The whole note fills the whole measure and receives all four counts.

Musicians often use the term "beat" to refer to the "count" in a piece of music. So when I say I want you to count evenly, what I mean in musician's terms, which you are rapidly becoming, is for you to keep a steady beat.

Look at the first row of notes below the whole note box. It consists of all of the notes you now know. The 1st measure contains 4 quarter notes; the 2nd measure includes 2 quarter notes and a half note; the 3rd measure is just like the 1st—4 quarter notes; and finally, the 4th measure contains our new note, the whole note, and there is just one because it is held for all 4 counts or beats. I would like you to clap and count the full line now. Clap once for each note, keeping your hands together on the half and whole notes, but count each beat aloud. Remember to keep a steady beat.

Count: 1, 1, 1, 1; 1, 1, 1-2; 1, 1, 1, 1; 1-2-3-4.

I would like you to repeat this exercise several times until you feel very comfortable clapping and counting quarter, half and whole notes.

AURA LEE

Aura Lee is a familiar and popular folk song. Elvis Presley once recorded a song called *Love Me Tender*, which is largely based on the melody of *Aura Lee*.

The only thing new in *Aura Lee* is the whole note in measures 4 and 8. Just remember to hold the key down for the full four counts, but do look ahead to measure 5 and be prepared to play the C with your 5th finger on the 1st count of that measure.

Read the 4 steps listed under the title, *Aura Lee*, then play each step one at a time. Go through each step several times until you feel comfortable and confident. Play with a moderate tone, not too soft or too loud. When you can play *Aura Lee* with a steady beat, you will have completed this page.

The Whole Note

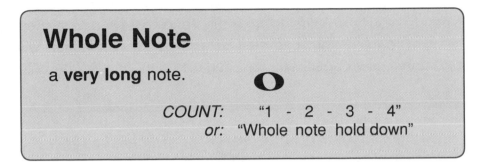

Whole Note

a **very long** note.

COUNT: "1 - 2 - 3 - 4"
       or: "Whole note hold down"

Clap (or tap) the following rhythm. Clap ONCE for each note, counting aloud.

AURA LEE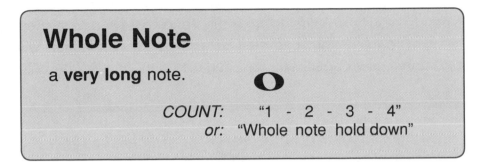

This melody was made into a popular song, *"LOVE ME TENDER,"* sung by Elvis Presley.

1. Clap (or tap) the rhythm, counting aloud.

2. Play & sing (or say) the finger numbers.

3. Play & count.

4. Play & sing (or say) the note names.

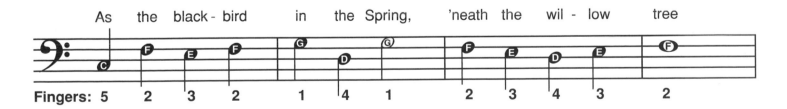

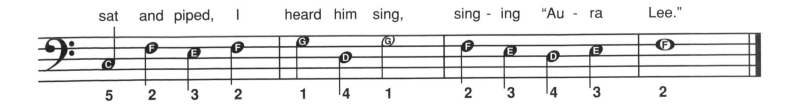

The Grand Staff

Now that you have learned how to read and play notes on the bass and treble staffs with the left and right hands, you are going to take the reading of music a step further. While you have been reading from one staff at a time, today's lesson will combine both staffs so that in a few pages, you can begin to play music with both hands at the same time.

Look at the large keyboard and music chart at the top of page 21. When the bass staff and the treble staff are joined together with a brace, it is called a *Grand Staff*. Positioning the staffs one over the other will allow you to play both hands together.

Just below the Grand Staff, the *Time Signature* is introduced. These are two numbers placed on the Grand Staff. The top number tells how many counts or beats are included in each measure and the bottom number tells what kind of note receives one beat.

In the example shown, the top 4 means there are 4 counts or beats in each measure; the bottom 4 means that a quarter note gets 1 count or beat. From now on, rather than count 1, 1, 1, 1 for each beat in $\frac{4}{4}$ time, you will count by the total beats within each measure: 1, 2, 3, 4.

PLAYING ON THE GRAND STAFF

This exercise on the bottom half of the page includes several new music symbols. Note the two $\frac{4}{4}$ time signatures following the treble and bass clefs. Also in the first measure, there is a sign of silence called a *rest* in the bass staff. A rest sign means you do not play for the length of the rest. The rest shown is a *whole rest*—it hangs down from the 4th line, and it means you do not play the LH for the whole measure. In measures 1 to 4, the RH plays alone and so the bass staff has a whole rest sign in each measure. In measures 5 to 8, the opposite occurs with the RH resting as the LH plays.

In measures 1 and 5, only the first note is fingered on each staff. Musicians read by recognizing on which line or space a note is placed, not by reading a finger number. For now, finger numbers can be helpful but in time, you will need them less and less as you learn to read music on the staff.

Finally, observe the double dots placed at the end of measure 8. This is a *repeat sign*. It simply means to go back to the beginning of this exercise and play it all the way through again without stopping. It's important to keep a steady beat when playing the 8th measure, and then go back to the 1st measure without pausing or missing a beat.

Alongside the title *Playing on the Grand Staff,* there are 3 practice procedures. This is a good way to prepare for every exercise and piece in this book. If there are no words, skip step 3. It may seem like it takes a little longer for you to do, but time will be saved in how quickly you will learn to play the music correctly.

The Grand Staff

The BASS STAFF and TREBLE STAFF, when joined together with a BRACE, make up the **GRAND STAFF.**

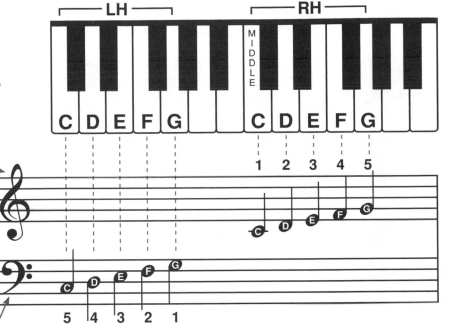

Treble Clef

Brace →

Bass Clef

TIME SIGNATURE

Music has numbers at the beginning called the **TIME SIGNATURE.**

4 means **4** beats to each measure.

4 means a **QUARTER NOTE** ♩ gets one beat.

PLAYING ON THE GRAND STAFF

Only the starting finger number for each hand is given.

The following practice procedure is recommended for the rest of the pieces in this book:

1. Clap (or tap) & count.
2. Play & count.
3. Play & sing the words, if any.

This sign ▬ is a **WHOLE REST.**
LH is silent a whole measure!

RH silent a whole measure.

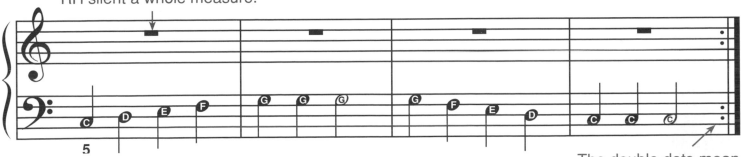

The double dots mean *repeat from the beginning.*

ROCK-ALONG

Rock-Along on page 23 contains nothing new but includes the time signature of $\frac{4}{4}$, the whole rest and the repeat sign, all introduced on page 21. Begin your practice by first clapping and counting, followed by playing and counting, the 2 steps listed in the recommended practice procedures on page 21. As there are no lyrics, skip the third step. Always remember to play with a steady beat. This is a fun piece that you will enjoy playing—but don't forget to observe the repeat sign at the end and go back to the beginning and play again.

MEXICAN HAT DANCE

Mexican Hat Dance is the introduction to a familiar piece. New in this piece is the *quarter rest*, introduced in the 1st measure. Rests, as you now know, are signs of silence. The quarter rest, just like the quarter note, receives 1 beat.

As this piece includes lyrics, practice by first clapping and counting, then playing and counting. Finally, play and sing (or say) the words, also called the *lyric*. You may find this a little uncomfortable at first but stay with it and it will be easier with each rendition. Many piano players are also singers and you may find that in the future, you will really enjoy singing while playing. By starting now, it will soon become a natural part of playing the piano.

After you are comfortable playing *Mexican Hat Dance,* you might also want to play *Rock-Along* and *Mexican Hat Dance* one right after the other, before turning the page.

ROCK-ALONG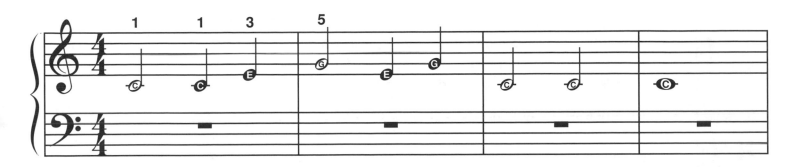

MEXICAN HAT DANCE

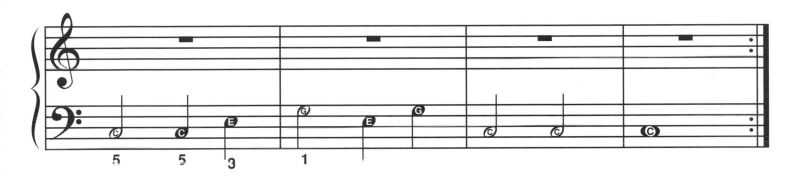

This sign 𝄽 is a QUARTER REST.
Rest for one count!

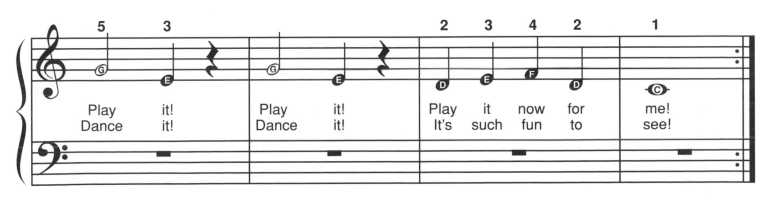

Melodic Intervals

With your ability now to read music on a Grand Staff, you will begin to study the structure of music, commonly referred to as *music theory*. The knowledge gained through music theory will ultimately lead to an understanding of how scales and chords are formed, the foundation of all music.

Distances between notes or tones are measured in intervals, such as 2nds, 3rds, 4ths, and 5ths. When notes are played separately, they create a *melody*, and so these notes are called *melodic intervals.* All melodies are made up of melodic intervals. When you played *Ode to Joy, Aura Lee, Rock-Along* and the *Mexican Hat Dance*, you were playing melodic intervals.

When you play a white key, then play the next white key whether up or down, the interval is called a 2nd. When you play a white key, skip the next white key, then play the 3rd white key, whether up or down, you are playing a 3rd. For now, you will play 2nds with fingers 1 and 2, and 3rds with fingers 1 and 3.

First read the text at the top of page 25, then play the top line of music. Note the repeat sign at the end of the line. Play this line several times and when you feel comfortable playing 2nds and 3rds, you will be ready for your next piece.

AU CLAIRE DE LA LUNE

On the second line of music is *Au claire de la lune*, a French folk song (in French, only the first word of a title is capitalized). It contains repeated notes and melodic 2nds and 3rds. Up until now, our study has not focused on how loud or soft the music was played. In written music, the level of sound is indicated by a *dynamic sign.* Italian words were first used when the language of music was developing and those same words are used today.

Read the text in the upper pink box and you will see an explanation for *dynamic signs*. *Piano* in Italian means *soft* and is indicated by a p in the music. When you play *Au claire de la lune* with your RH, play it softly. As the title means "by the light of the moon," playing softly seems like an appropriate dynamic level. There is a repeat sign at the end of the line that I want you to perform. Notice where the 2nds and 3rds are located before you play.

TISKET, A TASKET

The last song at the bottom of the page is *Tisket, a Tasket,* a children's song. Note the large mf in the lower pink box. *Mezzo forte (metso' for'tay)* in Italian means *moderately loud* and is indicated by an mf. Back in the 1930s, *Tisket, a Tasket* was recorded in a jazz style by Ella Fitzgerald. The recording became popular and helped establish Ella as one of the great singers in jazz history.

Tisket, a Tasket is played with the LH and is played a little louder than *Au claire de la lune*. Before performing this song, say the intervals between each of the notes. In measures 1 and 2, for example, say "3rd, 2nd, 2nd, 3rd, 2nd. It is always good practice to play through the entire page as a review before moving onto the next page.

Melodic Intervals

Distances between tones are measured in **INTERVALS,** called 2nds, 3rds, 4ths, 5ths, etc.

Notes played *separately* make a *melody.*
We call the intervals between these notes **MELODIC INTERVALS.**

Play these MELODIC 2nds & 3rds. Listen to the sound of each interval.

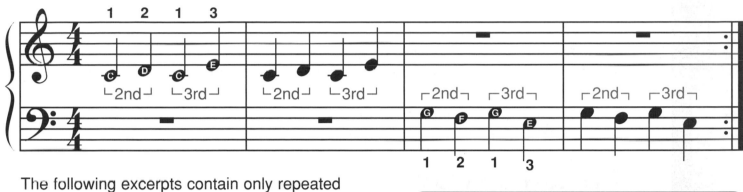

The following excerpts contain only repeated notes and MELODIC 2nds & 3rds.

AU CLAIRE DE LA LUNE

DYNAMIC SIGNS
tell how loud or
soft to play.

$\boldsymbol{p}$ *(piano)* = soft

TISKET, A TASKET

$\boldsymbol{mf}$ *(mezzo forte)* = moderately loud

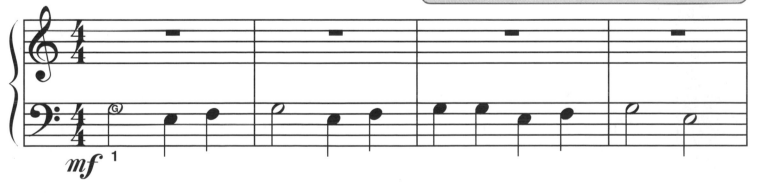

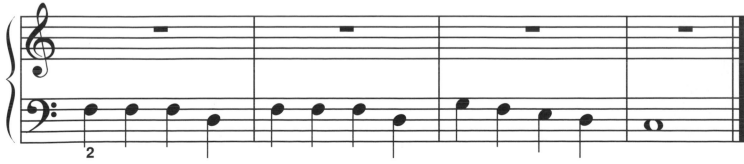

Harmonic Intervals

As you now know, a melody is made up of notes played one after the other and the intervals between those notes are called *melodic intervals*. When notes are played together, they create a sound called *harmony*, and so the intervals between those notes are called *harmonic intervals*. Look at the first line of music on page 27 and you will see examples of harmonic 2nds and 3rds.

Play the first line, saying 2nd or 3rd as you play the harmonic intervals. Listen as you play the intervals and see if you can hear the difference in sound between them. Remember that for now, you will play harmonic 2nds with fingers 1 and 2, and harmonic 3rds with fingers 1 and 3. Note the repeat sign at the end of the line. Also notice the music is played moderately loud, *mezzo forte*. After you have played this line a few times and feel ready to proceed, move on to *Rockin' Intervals*.

ROCKIN' INTERVALS

Rockin' Intervals, on the bottom half of the page, uses both *melodic* and *harmonic* intervals within one song. I think you will enjoy playing this piece very much.

New here, and located in the pink box, is another dynamic sign, the symbol for playing loud. It is called *forte* (*for'tay*) and the symbol used is an f. In the 2nd measure is a quarter rest which you learned when playing *Mexican Hat Dance* on page 23.

In measure 2, play the D with your RH on the 1st beat, then raise your hand slightly off the keyboard for the rest on the 2nd beat. On beat 3, play D again, and then raise your hand off the keyboard again on the 4th beat.

When you play *Rockin' Intervals*, I would like you to say "rest" whenever the quarter rest signs appear and "2nd" or "3rd" on the harmonic intervals. When playing *Rockin' Intervals*, you will play *forte,* or loud, for the first time. I don't want you to bang the keys—it really won't sound good. But definitely play it louder than you played the top exercise on this page. After playing *Rockin' Intervals* several times, review this page by playing it one more time.

The Duet Part at the bottom of the page is for a pianist or teacher to play along with you. A duet is when two musicians perform together at the same time. This is definitely worth doing if you have someone who can play piano. It will make the music sound very exciting. You're not a rock star yet, but you are on your way!

The piano was invented in the 1700s. Before the piano, there was the harpsichord. The way the harpsichord was constructed, musicians could only play at one sound level. The piano was an improvement because it could be played both soft and loud. Because of that, the new instrument was originally called the *pianoforte*, later shortened to just *piano*.

Harmonic Intervals

Notes played *together* make *harmony.*
We call the intervals between these notes **HARMONIC INTERVALS.**

Play these HARMONIC 2nds & 3rds. Listen to the sound of each interval.

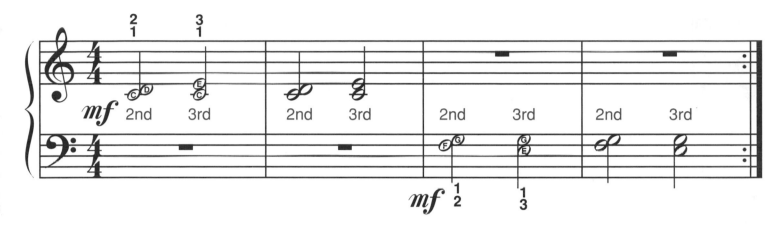

ROCKIN' INTERVALS

f *(torte)* = loud

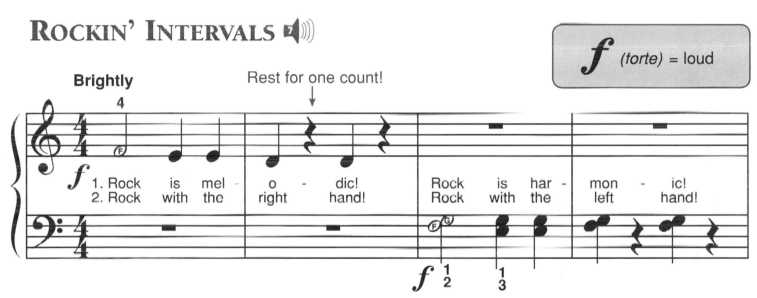

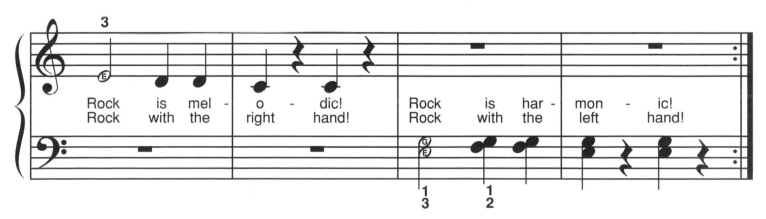

DUET PART FOR PIANIST OR TEACHER: (Student plays 1 octave higher.)

Melodic 4ths and 5ths

On pages 25 and 27, you learned to play intervals of a 2nd and a 3rd. On page 29, you will expand the intervals you can play to melodic 4ths and 5ths. Because of this, you will be able to perform many more songs and your performing skills will increase dramatically.

To play an interval of a 4th, you will skip 2 white keys. On the top line of music on page 29, in the first measure, the interval between the first 2 notes, C and F, is a 4th. C and F are separated by 2 white keys. To play an interval of a 5th, you will skip 3 white keys. Look at the next 2 notes in measure 1: C and G—that is an interval of a 5th. C and G are separated by 3 white keys.

For now, you will be playing the interval of a 4th with fingers 1 and 4, and the interval of a 5th with fingers 1 and 5. As you play the exercise on the top line, say 4th and 5th as you play the harmonic intervals. There is a repeat sign at the end of the line so play the first line again, this time counting 1, 2, 3, 4 for each measure. First place your right hand thumb on middle C, then your left hand thumb on bass note G and you're ready to begin.

When you can play the first line smoothly and evenly, you will be ready for your next piece.

GOOD KING WENCESLAS

Good King Wenceslas contains melodic 2nds and 4ths but, oddly enough, no 3rds. This should be played a little faster and a little louder than usual because the tempo marking says "Moderately fast" and the dynamic sign is *forte*. Before you begin, notice the interval of a 4th in the RH (it's in measure 2) and the interval of a 4th in the LH (it's in measure 6) so you won't be surprised as you play those measures. As you know everything in the music, you should have little trouble playing this well-known Christmas song.

MY FIFTH

My Fifth is the bottom song on the page. There is an interval of a 5th in the treble clef (between measures 1 and 2) and an interval of a 5th in the bass clef (between measures 5 and 6). The lyric is clever and contains a musical joke at the end. Ludwig van Beethoven was one of our greatest classical composers. He wrote 9 symphonies and they are numbered in the order in which Beethoven wrote them. His 5th Symphony is one of the most popular. What our little joke means is that the 5th Symphony actually begins with a series of melodic 3rds, which are the last 2 measures of the piece.

Read the second line of the lyric: "Beethoven's fifth is only a third." Also note that you are playing a 5th when you sing the word "fifth," and you are playing a 3rd when you sing the word "third."

Before you begin, look for the 5ths in the RH and the 5ths in the LH so you will know where they are located. All but the last 2 measures are played *piano*. Only the last 2 measures are played *forte*. When you feel comfortable playing *My Fifth*, I would like you to review this entire page by beginning at the top and playing right through to the end. Repeat this process as many times as you wish until you are completely comfortable playing the page.

Melodic 4ths & 5ths

Play these MELODIC 4ths & 5ths.
Listen to the sound of each interval.

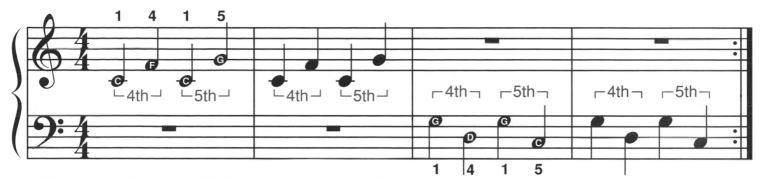

GOOD KING WENCESLAS 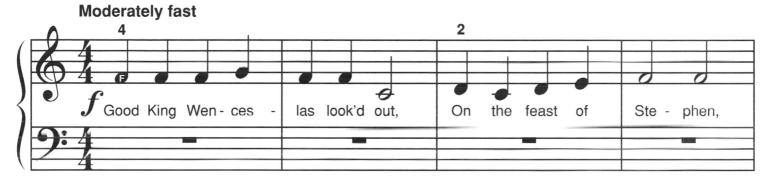 Find the 4ths before you play!

Moderately fast

Good King Wen - ces - las look'd out, On the feast of Ste - phen,

When the snow lay round a - bout, Deep and crisp and e - ven.

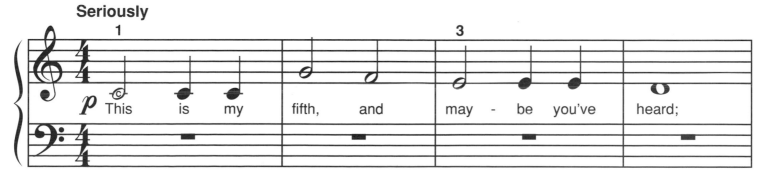

MY FIFTH 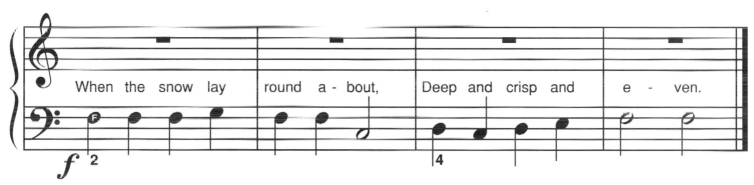 Find the 5ths before you play!

Seriously

This is my fifth, and may - be you've heard;

Beet - hov - en's fifth is on - ly a third!

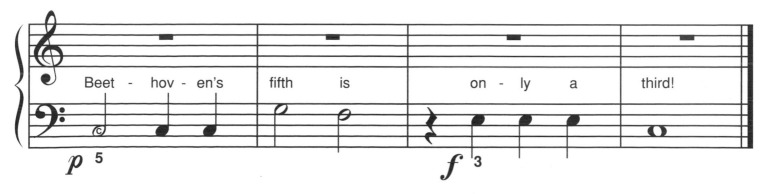

Harmonic 4ths & 5ths

As you know, a harmonic interval means the notes of the interval are played together. Playing harmonic intervals after you have mastered playing melodic intervals should present no new problems. What you should strive for is to play the notes absolutely together, not almost together.

Play *Harmonic 4ths & 5ths* on page 31 the same way you first played *Melodic 4ths & 5ths* on page 29. As you play, say the intervals, "4th, 5th" the first time and count 1, 2, 3, 4 on the repeat. There is a very big incentive for you to master the first line quickly because when you are ready, you will be learning how to play *Jingle Bells*, one of the most popular melodies ever written.

JINGLE BELLS

Jingle Bells is an amazing and wonderful song. Whatever the season, when you play it, it will feel like Christmas time in your heart. Watch for the melodic 4ths and 5ths in the RH, and the harmonic 4ths and 5ths in the LH.

The tempo *Merrily* means to play the song in a bright, lively tempo. The dynamic sign is *f* or *forte* so you will play loudly, but not too loud. I do not want you to bang the keys and risk hurting your fingers. When you can play *Jingle Bells* smoothly and evenly, try singing the lyrics as you play. When you can play and sing *Jingle Bells* easily, I have a very nice Christmas present for you. And what might that present be? Look under the piano and you will see a large box wrapped in silver paper with a bright red ribbon. Ah, if only I could. But actually, I have something even nicer for you.

Come Christmas time, invite some family members and friends over to your home and have them gather around the piano. First play *Jingle Bells* for them as a solo, then encourage them to sing along as you play *Jingle Bells* a second time. If they didn't know you were learning to play the piano, they will be pleased and surprised. If they did know, they will still be so proud of you and all will have a wonderful time. The memory of that moment is the best present I can give you and one I know you will never forget.

Harmonic 4ths & 5ths

Play these HARMONIC 4ths & 5ths.
Listen to the sound of each interval.

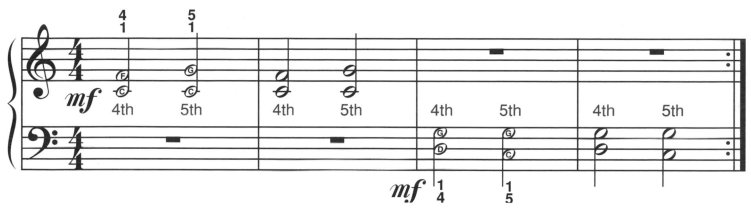

JINGLE BELLS

Before you play: 1. Find all the MELODIC 4ths & 5ths in the RH.
2. Find all the HARMONIC 4ths & 5ths in the LH.

Merrily

Jin - gle, bells! Jin - gle, bells! Jin - gle all the way!

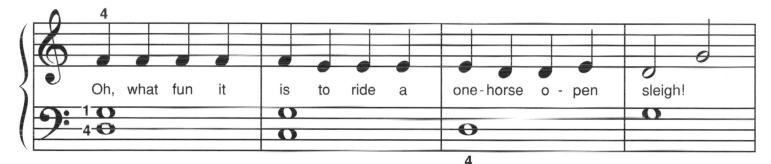

Oh, what fun it is to ride a one-horse o - pen sleigh!

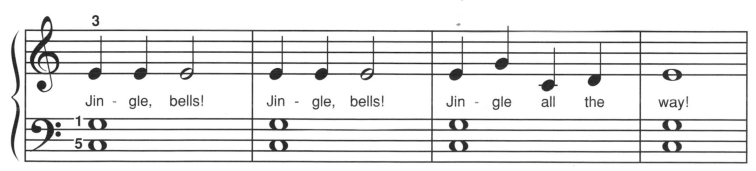

Jin - gle, bells! Jin - gle, bells! Jin - gle all the way!

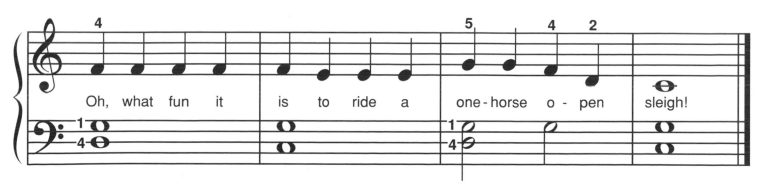

Oh, what fun it is to ride a one-horse o - pen sleigh!

You are going to learn something very important on page 33, and that is how to play a *chord*. When you played 2 notes together, you played an *interval*. When you can play 3 or more notes together, you are playing a *chord*.

Every chord has a letter-name, such as A, B, C; and a description, such as major, minor and seventh. They each are formed by a set of rules that we call *music theory,* and in time you will learn about some of them. For now, you should only be concerned with how to play the chord.

The C Major Chord

The first chord you will learn is the C major chord. The letter-name comes from the lowest of the three notes that form the chord. Look at the top of page 33 and to the right of the title, you will see a keyboard diagram placed over a music staff. Notice how the three notes on the bass staff, C-E-G, are stacked one on top of the other— that is what a chord looks like. The first chord you play will be with the LH.

Sitting at the piano, position your LH with the 5th finger on the C below middle C. While holding C down, add your 3rd finger on E, and your 1st finger on G. Try this now. Your fingers should be rounded to allow all of them to be the same length. Then, when you press the keys, the notes will all sound together.

Look at the keyboard diagram again and this time, play the C major chord with your RH. The RH plays the C chord almost as a mirror image of the LH except the fingers are reversed. Now the 1st finger of the RH is on middle C, the 3rd is on E, and the 5th is on G.

Play the LH C chord and lift your hand off the keys, then play the RH C chord and lift your hand off the keys. Repeat this procedure several times, listening to make sure the 3 keys are struck together to get a nice, clean chord sound.

C MAJOR CHORDS FOR LH

Look at the first complete line of music titled *C Major Chords for LH*. The dynamic sign *mf* or *mezzo forte* tells you to play this exercise moderately loud. As you already know the LH C major chord, play and count the exercise—the half notes receive 2 counts and the whole notes receive 4 counts. As there is a repeat sign at the end of the line, play it twice.

C MAJOR CHORDS FOR RH

The next lower line of music is titled *C Major Chords for RH*. Play the C major chords with your RH exactly as you played the chords with your LH. After playing this line, I would recommend you move up to the LH C chord line again and repeat that exercise; then repeat this RH C chord line exercise again.

C MAJOR CHORDS FOR BOTH HANDS

The bottom line contains nothing new except—and this is important—you are going to play chords with both hands playing together. This is not easy, but then again, it is not hard either. When you can play this line with a steady beat, you will be ready to play some melodies with chord accompaniments.

The C Major Chord

A chord is three or more notes played together.

The **C MAJOR CHORD** is made of three notes: **C E G.**

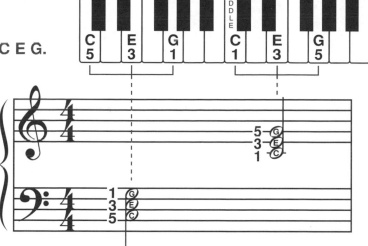

Be sure to play all three chord notes exactly together, with fingers nicely curved.

C MAJOR CHORDS FOR LH

Play & count.

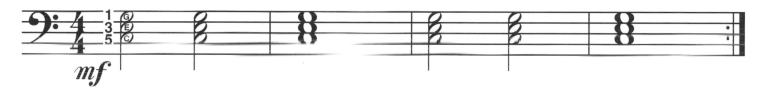

C MAJOR CHORDS FOR RH

Play & count.

C MAJOR CHORDS FOR BOTH HANDS

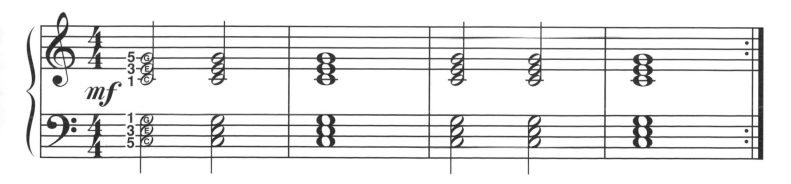

When approaching any new piece, if you first learn one hand, then learn the other, and then play with both hands together, you will likely learn to play the piece more quickly. I'd like you to begin to play *Brother John* on page 35 with this approach.

BROTHER JOHN

Brother John, also known as *Frère Jacques,* is a familiar folk song. Frére Jacques is a French title so why is the second word capitalized? Because it is a person's name. The *tempo marking* indicates to play this song *moderately fast*, but you do not have to start this way. The *dynamic sign* is *piano* so you will begin by playing *softly*. When you reach the beginning of the second line, you will now play *forte*, or *loudly*. What's new in this song is the introduction of the half rest in measures 7 and 8, the last two measures of the second line. It means to *rest* for two counts or beats.

Play *Brother John* 3 or 4 times. The only problem you might have is with the hand coordination in the last 2 measures of line 2. If you do, just isolate those measures and play them several times while counting. What I would really like to see happen is that you play *Brother John* so many times that you can actually play the song from memory without having to read the music. Then you can make music not only anytime, but anywhere there is a piano.

One of the really fun things to do while playing the piano is to be able to sing along. It is not possible to sing if you are having difficulty playing the music. Let's begin by singing *Brother John*. If you can perform *Brother John* easily, I want you to sing the lyrics as you play.

Playing and singing is an important skill to develop and by starting now, it will soon become second nature to you. Don't be concerned about how you sound. What is important is to just get used to singing while you play.

HERE'S A HAPPY SONG!

Notice the *f* or *forte* in the 1st measure so you will be playing the song *loudly*. One of the first things you should always do when learning a new piece is to look at the *tempo* and *dynamic* signs. Also notice the *repeat sign* at the end of the second line. After you learn to play this happy song, play the whole page, one song after the other. Sing the lyrics to *Brother John* as you play.

BROTHER JOHN

Moderately fast

> **Read by patterns!** For RH, think:
> "C, up a 2nd, up a 2nd, down a 3rd," etc.
> *Think* the pattern, then *play* it!

Are you sleep-ing,   Are you sleep-ing,   Broth-er John?   Broth-er John?

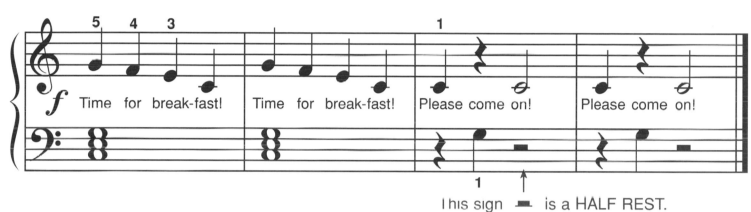

Time for break-fast!   Time for break-fast!   Please come on!   Please come on!

This sign 𝄼 is a HALF REST.
Rest for two counts!

HERE'S A HAPPY SONG!

> **Read by patterns!** For LH, think:
> "G, down a 2nd, down a 2nd," etc.

Happily

Introducing (B) for Left hand

Up until this page, you have played all the music within a range of 5 notes. With the addition of B in the LH, you will now expand that range to 6 notes. Look at the keyboard chart at the top of page 37 and while sitting at the piano, place your LH over the C position with your 5th finger on C. This C position is below middle C. Now extend your 5th finger to the left, down to B below C. On the staff above the keyboard chart, notice that this B is written on the second line of the bass staff.

While holding your LH in the C position, move your 5th finger several times between C and B. Try to not move your hand, just your finger. When you feel comfortable doing this, play the first line of music on page 37. It's a little bit of a stretch but I don't think you will find this difficult. There is a repeat sign at the end of the line so play the music several times. Say the finger numbers the first time, the letter names the second time, and count the 3rd time. Notice the time signature is in $\frac{4}{4}$ time. When you can play this line fairly easily, you are ready to learn to play a new chord, the G7 chord.

Two Important Chords

You already are familiar with the LH C chord, and now you will add the G7 chord to your repertoire. With the addition of this new chord, you will be able to play music that is a little more complex and much more interesting. You have already played the G7 chord as single notes in the exercise on line 1 in measure 2.

Look at the keyboard chart on the lower left side of the page and play the C major chord. While holding your fingers on the C chord, play the G7 chord that is diagrammed on the keyboard chart to the right of the C major chord.

To change from playing the C chord to the G7 chord, first hold your fingers over C-E-G. The top note G in the C chord is the same top note of the G7 chord. While holding G down, lift your 3rd finger off E and press down the F key below G with the 2nd finger. Finally, move your 5th finger from C to the B below C and you are in position to play the G7 chord. Try playing the C and G7 chords, going back and forth several times. I think you will find this fun to do.

Review the text at the bottom of the page that describes the process of changing chords. When you can move easily from one chord to the next, play the little musical exercise at the bottom of the page several times until you feel comfortable.

Why this chord is called the G7 chord is not too complicated. Music theory is a fascinating subject and later on page 129 you will learn why this chord is called a G7 chord. For now, you will only need to know that G7 is its name.

Introducing ⓑ for Left Hand

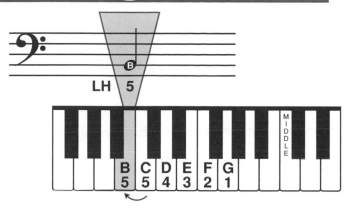

TO FIND B:

Place the LH in **C POSITION.**
Reach finger 5 one white key to the left!

Play slowly. Say the note names as you play.

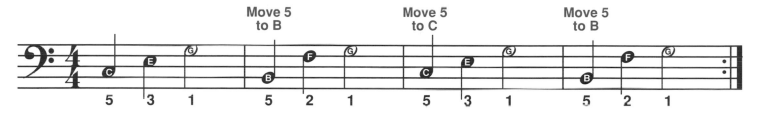

Two Important Chords

Two frequently used chords are **C MAJOR** & **G⁷.**

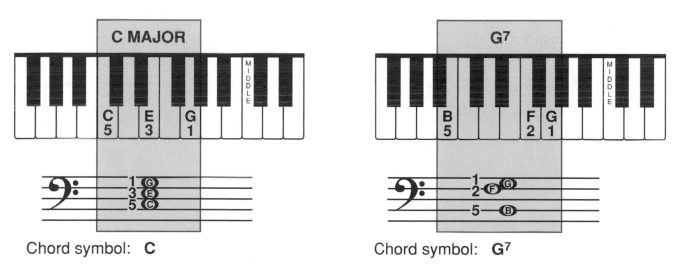

Chord symbol: **C**   Chord symbol: **G⁷**

Chord symbols are always used in popular music to identify chord names.

Practice changing from the C chord to the G⁷ chord and back again:

1. The 1st finger plays G in both chords.
2. The 2nd finger plays F in the G⁷ chord.
3. Only the 5th finger moves out of C POSITION (down to B) for G⁷.

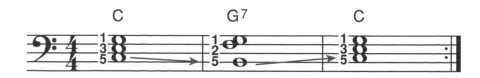

Tied Notes

At the top of page 39, you will see an explanation of *Tied Notes*. Tied notes extend notes beyond their normal counts. By using curved lines, 2 notes can be joined together. To the right of the top paragraph, you will see what I mean. Hold any note down with your RH and count one measure. Then, without lifting your hand, count the next measure. The combined value of the 2 whole notes is 8 but we don't count it that way, we count 1-2-3-4, 1-2-3-4. Tied notes have to be on the same line or space.

MERRILY WE ROLL ALONG

Look at *Merrily We Roll Along*, measures 1 and 2. The LH plays the C chord and holds it for 2 measures because the notes are tied. *Merrily We Roll Along* should be familiar to you as it is a very popular children's song. Because the melody is in the RH, it should be played a little louder than the LH. Note the *mf* below the first RH note in the treble staff and the *p* below the first LH chord in the bass staff.

Other than the tied notes, there is nothing new in this piece. The LH part is called the *accompaniment*. It gets this name because it accompanies and supports the melody in the RH. Not all pieces you play will be just melody and accompaniment, but when you do play such a piece, always play the melody part a little louder.

Notice the chord symbols C and G7 placed above the treble staff. In popular sheet music, they appear above the RH melody part. They are not written each time the chord is played, only when there is a chord change, as in measures 3 and 4. Now play *Merrily We Roll Along* quite a few times until you can play it evenly and musically. To help you become more familiar with the chords, say the name of each chord as you play them.

LARGO

The bottom piece on this page is *Largo*. It was composed by Antonin Dvoůák and it is from his most popular work, the Ninth Symphony "*From the New World.*" Dvoůák was born near Prague in what is now the Czech Republic in 1841. He spent most of his life there except for the years 1892 to 1895 when he lived in New York City. While there he composed his *New World Symphony*. The second movement was so reminiscent of a spiritual that lyrics were written for it and it became better known as *Going Home*. You should have no problems with *Largo* but make sure to play it slowly. As you play, say the name of each chord.

TIED NOTES: When notes on the *same* line or space
are joined with a curved line, we call them *tied notes*.

The key is held down for the
COMBINED VALUES OF BOTH NOTES!

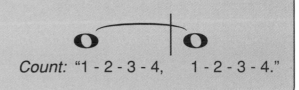

Count: "1 - 2 - 3 - 4,   1 - 2 - 3 - 4."

MERRILY WE ROLL ALONG 🔊

Play the RH & LH separately at first, then together. Practice the RH *mf* and the LH *p*.
The melody should always be clearly heard above the accompaniment.

LARGO *(from "The New World")* 🔊

This melody is also known as *GOING HOME*.

Dvořák

*In most popular sheet music, the chord symbols appear ABOVE the RH melody.
The symbol appears ONLY WHEN THE CHORD CHANGES.

Introducing Ⓑ for Right Hand

Now it is the right hand's turn to expand its range of notes from 5 to 6 and to learn to play the G7 chord. Page 41 is almost a mirror image of page 37. The fingerings are slightly different because of the change of hands but other than that the pages are very similar.

Look at the keyboard chart at the top of the page 41 and while sitting at the piano, place your RH over the C position with your 1st finger on C. Without moving your hand, move your 1st finger one key to the left, down to the B below middle C.

While holding your RH in the C position, move your 1st finger several times between C and B. Try to not move your hand, just your finger. When you feel comfortable doing this, play the first line of music on page 41. There is a repeat sign at the end of the line so play the music twice. Say the finger numbers the first time and the letter names on the repeat. When you can play this line easily, you are ready to learn to play the G7 chord with the RH.

C & G7 Chords for Right Hand

Look at the keyboard chart on the lower left side of the page and play the C major chord. While holding your fingers on the C chord, play the G7 chord that is diagrammed on the keyboard chart to the right of the C chord.

To change from playing the C chord to the G7 chord, first hold your fingers over C-E-G. The top note G in the C chord is the same top note of the G7 chord. While holding G down with your 5th finger, lift your 3rd finger off the E key and press down the F key below G with the 4th finger. Finally, move your 1st finger from the C to the B below C and you are in position to play the G7 chord. Try playing the C and G7 chords, going back and forth several times.

Review the text at the bottom of the page that describes the process of changing chords. When you can move easily from one chord to the next, play the little musical exercise at the bottom of the page several times until you feel comfortable.

Self-Teaching Study Guide

Introducing (B) for Right Hand

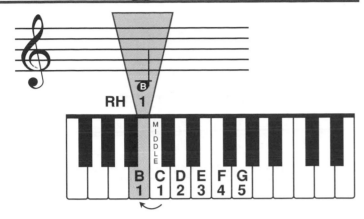

TO FIND B:

Place the RH in **C POSITION.**
Reach finger 1 one white key to the left!

Play slowly. Say the note names as you play.

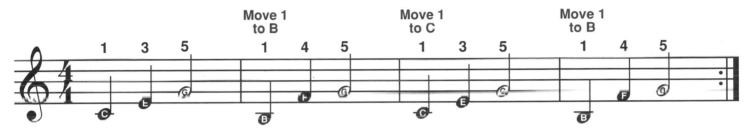

C & G⁷ Chords for Right Hand

It is very important to be able to play all chords with the RIGHT hand as well as the LEFT.
Chords are used in either or both hands in popular and classical music.

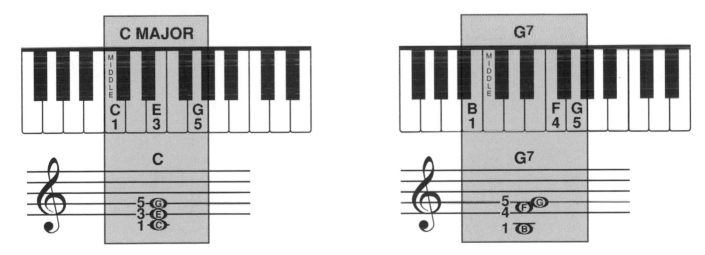

Practice changing from the C chord to the G⁷ chord and back again:

1. The 5th finger plays G in both chords.
2. The 4th finger plays F in the G⁷ chord.
3. Only the 1st finger moves out of C POSITION (down to B) for G⁷.

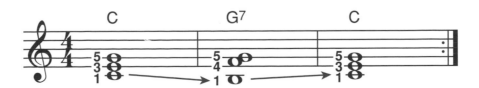

MARY ANN

Mary Ann on page 43 is a wonderful Calypso song that is fun to play and sing. What's a little different about this arrangement is that the melody is played by the LH and the chord accompaniment is played by the right. Because you want the melody to stand out, play the LH a little louder, *mezzo forte*, and the RH a little softer, *piano*. Look at the *mf* under the bass note in the 1st measure, and the *p* over the first note in the 4th measure.

In measure 6 on the second line, the LH 5 extends down to B, just as it does when playing the G7 chord. You will have to stretch a little to then go to the next note D with the 4th finger. You might want to play the second line with the LH alone to get the feel of it. The same thing appears again on the bottom line of the music.

One approach to learning this piece would be to practice *Mary Ann* by first playing the complete song with the LH alone. It will then be a simple matter to add the RH C and G7 chords at the end of each line. Notice the chord symbols above the chords which tell you the chord names.

It's always helpful to count aloud evenly as you practice to make certain you are maintaining the proper tempo. Some students tend to rush playing the chords at the end of each line so it is important to count evenly to prevent this. After you can play *Mary Ann* smoothly, sing along as you play. The lyrics in parentheses mean to sing those words a little softer, like an echo effect.

That's all there is to it so see how quickly you can learn to play *Mary Ann*. As you play, imagine you are on a beach on one of the Caribbean islands with palm trees swaying all around you and see how much more fun playing Calypso music can really be.

MARY ANN

Calypso tune

Moderately fast

All day, all night, Ma - ry Ann, (Ma - ry Ann,)

Down by the sea - shore, sift - in' sand; (sift - in' sand;)

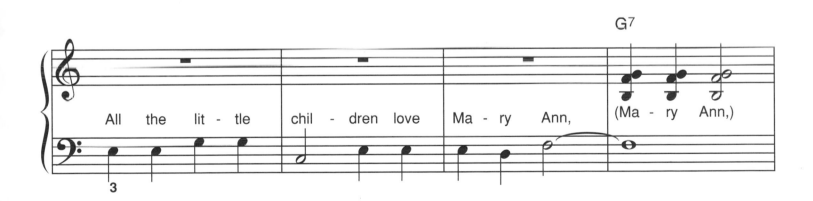

All the lit - tle chil - dren love Ma - ry Ann, (Ma - ry Ann,)

Down by the sea - shore, sift - in' sand. (sift - in' sand.)

New Time Signature and Dotted Half Notes

All of the pieces you have played so far have been counted 1-2-3-4, 1-2-3-4, known as $\frac{4}{4}$ time. Many melodies lend themselves to this time signature. But when you play music in $\frac{3}{4}$ time, you get a slightly different feel and rhythm. Look at the top left box on page 45 to see the new $\frac{3}{4}$ time signature. The count will now be 1-2-3, 1-2-3, with a quarter note still receiving one beat. Look at the top right box on page 45 and you will see a new note, the dotted half note. While a whole note is held for four beats or a whole measure in $\frac{4}{4}$ time, the dotted half note will be held for three beats or a whole measure in $\frac{3}{4}$ time. The dot extends the time of any note by one half.

Clap the rhythm pattern of the top line of music and count 1-2-3, 1-2-3 as you clap. Because there is a repeat sign at the end of the line, clap and count twice. Hold your hands together as you count 1-2-3 for the dotted half notes.

ROCKETS

Rockets is the first piece you will play in $\frac{3}{4}$ time. Notice that the first line has an f for **forte** so play the line *louder*. The second line has a p for **piano** so play the second line *softer*.

Also, at the bottom of the page is some text with the word *Important!* written to the left. It suggests that when you can play *Rockets* smoothly, play it again but after you play the first line, play the second line one octave (8 notes) higher. The word *octave* is derived from the Latin word *octavas,* meaning 8. Finally, play *Rockets* one more time, but this time play the first line one octave higher than written, and then play the second line two octaves higher than written. This is very good training in moving your hands freely over the keyboard. Just imagine the rocket going higher and higher as you play.

I would suggest that you first practice this piece by playing the music without the LH chords, counting 1-2-3, 1-2-3. Then, just play the chords alone—a G7 chord going to a C chord two times. Do you see the chord symbols above the music? Finally, put the two hands together.

New Time Signature

Dotted Half Note

3 means **3** beats to each measure.

4 means a **QUARTER NOTE** ♩ gets one beat.

A **DOTTED HALF NOTE** gets 3 counts.
(2 counts for the half note,
plus 1 count for the dot!) 𝅗𝅥·

COUNT: "1 - 2 - 3"

Clap (or tap) the following rhythm.

Clap **ONCE** for each note, counting aloud.

$\frac{3}{4}$ ♩ ♩ ♩ | 𝅗𝅥· | ♩ ♩ ♩ | 𝅗𝅥· :‖

1   2   3   1 - 2 - 3

ROCKETS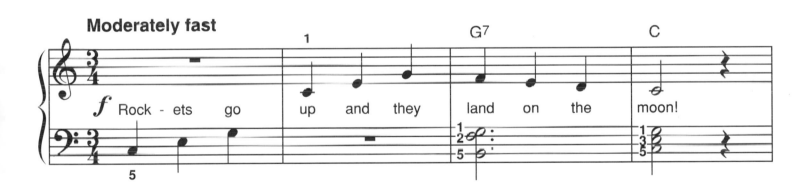

Moderately fast

IMPORTANT! Play *ROCKETS* again, playing the second line one octave (8 notes) higher. The rests at the end of the first line give you time to move your hands to the new position!

Play *ROCKETS* one more time, now with the first line one octave higher than written, and the second line two octaves higher.

This is excellent training in moving freely over the keyboard!

Slurs & Legato Playing

On page 47, you will learn something new about playing the piano. At the top of the page, you will see a long curved line. It is called a *slur* and it goes over or under notes that are on *different* lines or spaces. A tie, you remember, connects only the *same* notes. Look through the music of *What Can I Share?* and you will see 4 long slurs, one on each line. These slurs are all *over* the notes. Slurs indicate that the notes are to be played smoothly connected or *legato*. In the last 2 measures of the piece, you will see a C tied to another C in the treble clef—these are *tied* notes.

A slur groups notes together almost like a sentence. When you speak, you unconsciously pause at the end of each sentence, which serves to group your thoughts together. Music is somewhat similar. A series of notes with a slur is a musical thought or expression that has a natural flow. By performing the slurs properly and smoothly connecting the notes, you will be playing much more musically and will be well on your way to becoming a good pianist and musician.

WHAT CAN I SHARE?

Start your practice of *What Can I Share?* by playing the bass notes on the first and second lines, which are the melody notes. Group the slurred notes smoothly together. As this is a love song, play it *moderately slow*. Count the 3 beats in each measure evenly, 1-2-3, 1-2-3.

In the third and fourth lines, the melody shifts from the LH to the RH. When you complete the bottom 2 lines by playing the treble notes only, play the complete melody while counting. The LH plays lines 1 and 2, the RH plays lines 3 and 4. Play them several times before adding the other hand.

After you can play the melody lines easily, the only thing left to do is to add the chords. In lines 1 and 2, the RH plays the C chord, followed by the G7 chord, followed by the C chord. In lines 3 and 4, the LH plays the C, G7, and C chords. You've played these chords before so it should not present a problem for you. In the bottom line, next to the last measure, notice the word *slower*. This means to gradually slow down as you play the last 2 measures.

Don't forget to play the melody lines slightly louder than the chord accompaniment. When you can play the song easily, sing the lyrics as you play. You will now be doing a lot of things at once. Not only is it enjoyable in itself but it is a good mental exercise. It's a musical way of multi-tasking.

Slurs & Legato Playing

A **SLUR** is a curved line over or under notes on *different* lines or spaces.

SLURS mean play **LEGATO** (smoothly connected).

Slurs often divide the music into PHRASES.

A PHRASE is a musical thought or sentence.

WHAT CAN I SHARE?

Moderately slow

What can I share   with   you
To show my love   is   true?
Love's all we   need   to   share
To show how much   we   care!   *slower*

On page 49, you are again going to expand the notes you can play with the LH, but instead of moving down to B from the C position, we are going to move up to A from the C position.

Introducing (A) for Left Hand

Look at the keyboard chart at the top of page 49 and while sitting at the piano, place your LH over the C position with your 1st finger over G. This C position is below middle C. Without moving your hand, move your 1st finger one key to the right, up to A below middle C. On the staff above the keyboard chart, notice that this A is written on the 5th or top line of the bass staff.

While holding your LH in C position, move your 1st finger several times between G and A. Try to not move your hand, just your finger. When you feel comfortable doing this, play the first line of music on page 49. There is a repeat sign at the end of the line so play the music twice. Say the finger numbers the first time and the letter names on the repeat. When you can play this line easily, you are ready to learn to play the F major chord with the LH. Notice the time signature is in $\frac{4}{4}$ time now.

Introducing the F Major Chord

You are now ready to learn to play another important chord, the F major chord. You already are familiar with the LH C major chord. Look at the keyboard charts on the lower half of the page and place your LH hand over the keys of the C chord with your 5th finger on C.

Now look at the keyboard chart to the right, the F major chord. C is the bottom note of both the C and F chords so keep your 5th finger on C. Then shift your 3rd and 5th fingers one key to the right, up to F and A. You are now fingering the F major chord. Play the C chord, then play the F chord, going back and forth between the two chords several times.

Read the text at the bottom of the page, and practice playing the C and F chords by playing the bottom line of music over and over.

Introducing 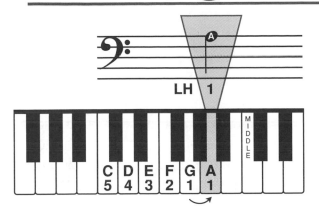 for Left Hand

TO FIND A:

Place the LH in **C POSITION**.
Reach finger 1 one white key to the right!

Play slowly. Say the note names as you play.

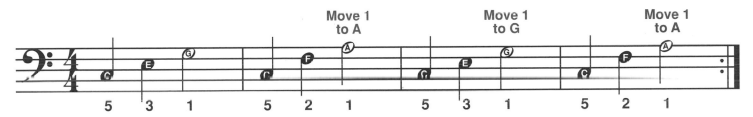

Introducing the F Major Chord

The C MAJOR chord is frequently followed by the F MAJOR chord, and vice-versa.

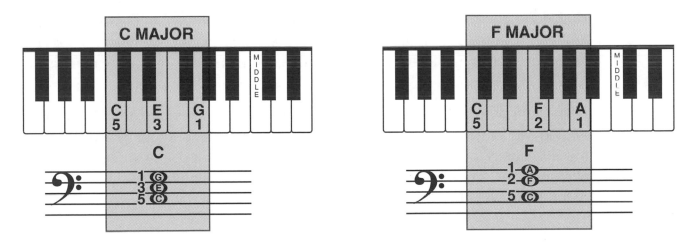

Practice changing from the C chord to the F chord and back again:

1. The 5th finger plays C in both chords.
2. The 2nd finger plays F in the F chord.
3. Only the 1st finger moves out of C POSITION (up to A) for the F chord.

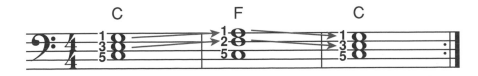

Warm-Up using C, G7 & F Chords

We now have a big treat for you. On page 51, you are going to learn to play the very popular *When the Saints Go Marching In*. If you've ever been to New Orleans, then you know the excitement this song can create whenever a Dixieland band performs it.

But before you can play *When the Saints Go Marching In*, you will have to learn to play the 3 LH chords that you already know, C, G7 and F, together in one piece. The top music line is an exercise that will give you the opportunity to do just that. When you play the top line, say the name of the chord at the beginning of each measure. When you can play this exercise and its 3 chords with ease, you are ready to play that great and wonderful Dixieland melody.

WHEN THE SAINTS GO MARCHING IN

Not all measures at the beginning of a song have the complete number of beats that the time signature calls for. When 1 or more beats are missing, the measure is called an *incomplete measure*. The missing beat or beats will be found in the very last measure of the piece. But first read the text in the pink box to the right of the title.

Because there is a repeat sign in the last measure, when you play the LH C chord you will continue, without missing a beat, to the 3 notes in the 1st measure and play the whole song through again. As the 1st measure has only 3 beats, begin to play on count 2. Songs that begin with an incomplete measure, therefore, never begin on the first count. In *When the Saints Go Marching In*, begin with 4 counts, then one more count, then play: 1-2-3-4, 1-(play).

Notice the chord symbols above the music which tell you what chord is being played in that measure. Look at the C chord symbol above the first complete measure—this chord continues until you see a different chord symbol (the last measure in line 2). This process repeats itself throughout the song.

Begin your practice by playing the RH alone, then the LH alone, then hands together, ending with playing hands together as you sing. Remember to play the melody line in the RH slightly louder than the chord accompaniment. And very importantly, when you play the LH C chord in the last measure on count 1, play the RH C at the beginning of the song on count 2 without hesitation.

Warm-Up using C, G⁷ & F Chords

Practice SLOWLY at first, then gradually increase speed.

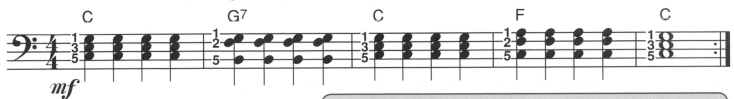

WHEN THE SAINTS GO MARCHING IN
(With RH MELODY & LH CHORDS)

> **INCOMPLETE MEASURE**   Some pieces begin with an *incomplete measure*. The first measure of this piece has only 3 counts. The missing count is found in the last measure! When you repeat the whole song, you will have one whole measure of 4 counts when you play the last measure plus the first measure.

March time

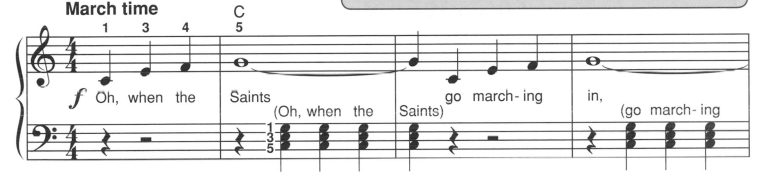

Oh, when the Saints go march-ing in, (go march-ing
(Oh, when the Saints)

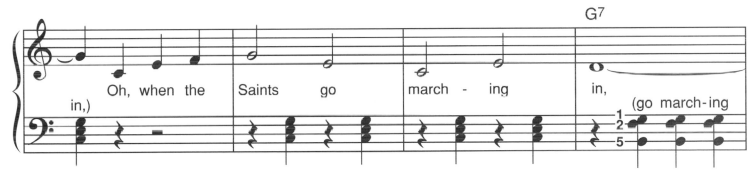

Oh, when the Saints go march - ing in, (go march-ing
in,)

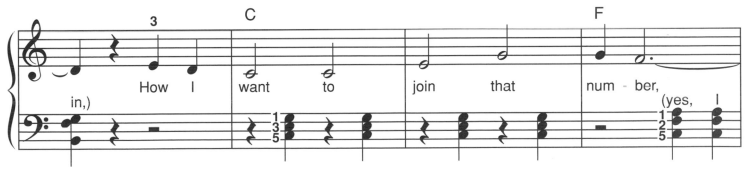

How I want to join that num - ber, (yes, I
in,)

When the Saints go march - ing in! (go march-ing in!)
do,)

On page 53, you are going to expand the range of the RH by moving up one note from the C position. This is very similar to what you learned on page 49 for the LH.

Introducing (A) for Right Hand

Look at the keyboard chart at the top of page 53 and while sitting at the piano, place your RH over the C position with your 1st finger on C. Now shift fingers 2, 3, 4, and 5, one key to the right, up to E, F, G and A. On the staff above the keyboard chart, notice that this A is written in the second space of the treble staff. Now shift fingers 2, 3, 4 and 5 back down to D, E, F and G. Do this several times. When you feel comfortable doing this, play the first music line several times, saying the finger numbers the first time, the letter names the second time, and counting on the third. The musical example is in $\frac{4}{4}$ time.

C & F Chords for Right Hand

You are now ready to learn to play the F major chord with the RH. You already are familiar with the RH C chord. Look at the keyboard charts on the lower half of the page and place your RH over the keys of the C chord with your 1st finger on C.

Now look at the keyboard chart to the right, the F major chord. C is the bottom note of both the C and F chords so keep your 1st finger on C. Then shift your 3rd and 5th fingers one key to the right, up to F and A. You are now fingering the F major chord. Play the C chord, then play the F chord, going back and forth between the two chords several times.

Read the text at the bottom of the page, and practice playing the C and F chords by playing the bottom line of music over and over.

Introducing Ⓐ for Right Hand

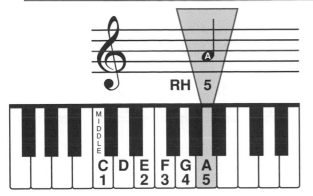

RH 5

TO FIND A:

Place the RH in **C POSITION.**
Leave 1 on C.
Shift all other fingers one white key to the right!

Play slowly. Say the note names as you play.

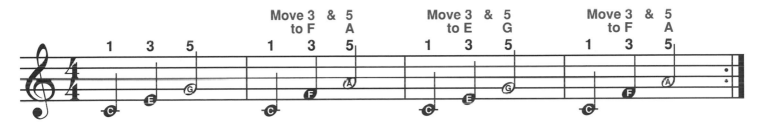

C & F Chords for Right Hand

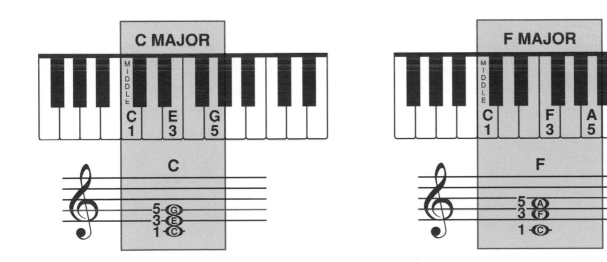

Practice changing from the C chord to the F chord and back again:

1. The 1st finger plays C in both chords.
2. The 3rd finger moves up to F and the 5th finger moves up to A for the F chord.

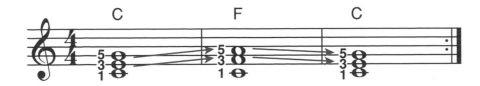

Warm-Up using C, G7 & F Chords

As on page 51, you will first learn to play the 3 RH chords that you already know, C, G7 and F, together in one piece. The top line of music on page 55 is an exercise that will give you the opportunity to do just that. When you play the top line, say the name of the chord at the beginning of each measure. When you can play this exercise and its 3 chords easily, you are ready to learn a different version of *When the Saints Go Marching In*.

WHEN THE SAINTS GO MARCHING IN

Notice that the 1st measure of the *Saints* is an incomplete measure, same as before. As the piece is in $\frac{4}{4}$ time, this means you will begin playing on the 2nd beat of the first incomplete measure. The missing beat from that 1st measure is found in the very last measure.

When you practice this piece, I want you to start by playing the LH alone, then the RH alone, and then hands together. What's different about this version is that the melody line is in the LH and the accompaniment is in the RH. It's more common the other way around but this version makes for an interesting variation. It also means you will play the LH slightly louder than your right. This may be a little difficult at first but the more you play the *Saints*, the better you will get at it. Notice the chord symbols above the music which will be your chord guide—but it is better to learn to recognize the chords by reading the music.

When you can play this version as easily as the one on page 51, read the text at the bottom of the page and play both versions one after the other. The trick is playing the second version right after the first without stopping, that is playing page 51 followed by page 55. As turning the pages will take a little time, see if you can memorize the second version so you can play the whole arrangement without stopping.

Most pianists memorize a number of pieces so when called upon to play at another location, they can sit down and entertain. Try memorizing both versions of *When the Saints Go Marching In* so you can play them both without stopping. See how proud you will feel about yourself and how pleased others will be with you when you perform.

Warm-Up using C, G⁷ & F Chords

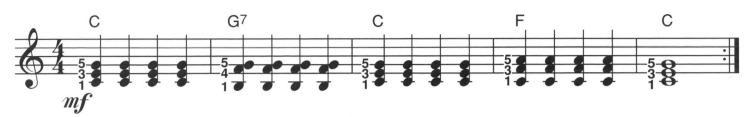

WHEN THE SAINTS GO MARCHING IN

(With LH MELODY & RH CHORDS)

After you have learned both versions of *WHEN THE SAINTS GO MARCHING IN,* you will find it very effective to play page 51 followed immediately by page 55. Instead of playing the piece one way and repeating, you will be playing the melody first in the RH, then in the LH!

Until now, you have played in only one position—the C position. In the early stages of learning, playing is limited to just a small span of notes. As you progress, you will be widening that span until finally, you won't be playing in positions at all.

The piano is a most remarkable instrument. It has a larger range of notes than most other instruments. There are a total of 88 keys on the piano and by learning more positions, you will be using more of these keys. Wind instruments have a more difficult time playing very low and very high notes. On the piano, all keys are just as easy to play, from the lowest to the highest. That is one reason why the piano is so remarkable.

G Position

Look at the top of page 57 and you will see the keyboard chart and grand staff of the G position. Sitting at the piano, place your LH 5th finger on the G below middle C—then let fingers 4–3–2–1 come to rest on A–B–C–D. Next, place your RH 1st finger on the G above middle C, 8 notes or one octave higher than the lower G—then let fingers 2–3–4–5 come to rest on A–B–C–D. That is the G position.

The first half-line of music has a single staff, with the bass staff first. Play the LH G position alone saying the note names, first going up and then coming down. Next, play the second half-line of music with the RH in G position saying the note names, first going up and then coming down. Familiarize yourself with the notes on the staff. Study the top keyboard chart and, in particular, learn the letter names of the notes and where they are positioned.

Intervals in G Position

The grand staff under *Intervals in G Position* includes only melodic intervals, single notes that are played individually. Say the name of each melodic interval as you play this exercise several times.

The bottom line includes only harmonic intervals, notes that are played together. Say the name of each harmonic interval as you play this exercise several times. Notice there are only half notes in each of these measures so each interval will receive two counts. If you can play these two lines easily while being able to say the letter names on the upper staff and the harmonic intervals on the lower staff, the next page will be very easy for you to learn.

G Position

Until now you have played
only in the C POSITION.

Now you will move to the G POSITION:

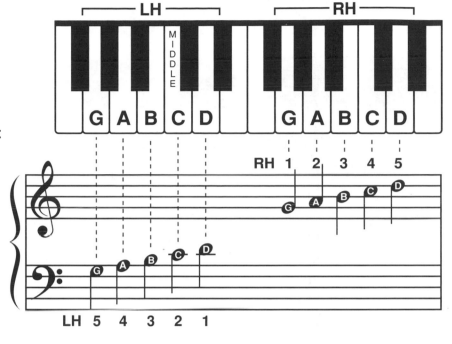

RH 1 on the G above middle C.

LH 5 on the G below middle C.

Play and say the note names. Be sure to do this SEVERAL TIMES!

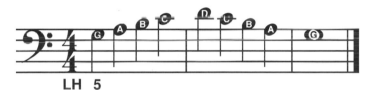

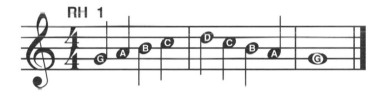

Intervals in G Position

1. MELODIC INTERVALS

Say the name of each interval as you play.

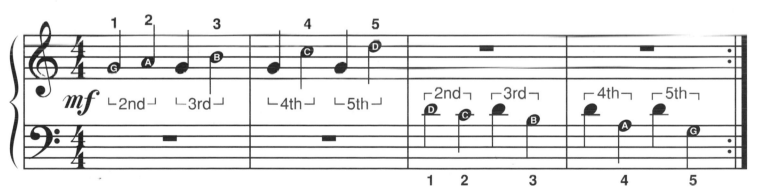

2. HARMONIC INTERVALS

Say the name of each interval as you play.

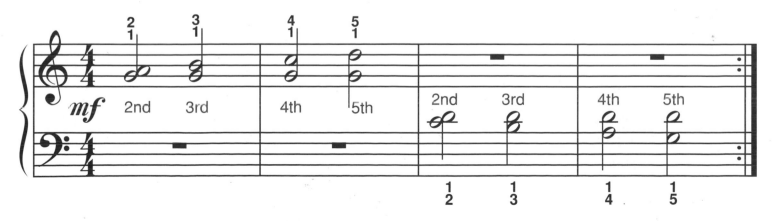

LOVE SOMEBODY

Love Somebody, on page 59, is a familiar folk song. Before beginning to play any new piece, it is always a good idea to look over the music before you start. Notice that *Love Somebody* is played "Happily" so it will move along at a nice pace. Following the ***f-p*** in the 1st measure, you will see the words "1st time ***f***, 2nd time ***p***." That means you will play the music *loud* the first time and *soft* on the repeat.

I would recommend you learn this piece by first playing the RH alone and when you can do that well, play the LH alone saying the harmonic intervals as you play (2nd, 3rd, 4th), and finally, playing both hands together. You might also try isolating measures 2, 4, 6 and 8, playing them with hands together. As both hands are playing in opposite directions in those measures, you might want to concentrate on them a little more. Other than that, you should have no trouble playing this very pleasant folk song.

A FRIEND LIKE YOU

A Friend Like You is an original piece, written just for this course and it is very appealing. Many of my students really like this piece and I hope you do also. Look at the music first and notice it is played "Moderately slow." It begins with an incomplete measure starting on the 2nd count. Sure enough, there is the missing 1st count in the last measure of the bottom line. Notice the text in red under that incomplete last measure. It says that on the repeat, you will move the LH one octave or 8 notes lower. It's an interesting variation that is fun to play.

Once again, start your practice by playing the RH alone, then playing the LH alone while naming each harmonic interval as you play (5th, 4th, 3rd, 4th, 5th). The LH part is a little more complicated than *Love Somebody*. Notice in the first line, first complete measure, the LH begins with a harmonic 5th, and in the last measure of the first line, the LH begins with a harmonic 4th. In the bottom line, the LH in the 2nd measure also begins with a harmonic 4th, but in the last complete measure, the LH begins with a harmonic 5th. You will be ready to move on when you can play *A Friend Like You* while singing the lyrics. Better still, sing it to a friend you really like.

LOVE SOMEBODY! 20))))

Before playing hands together, play LH alone, naming each harmonic interval!

A FRIEND LIKE YOU 21))))

Before playing hands together, play LH alone, naming each harmonic interval!

Repeat with LH
one octave (8 notes) lower.

THE DONKEY

The Donkey on page 61 is a *round.* It is a well-known piece and you may be familiar with it. The round is an interesting musical form. After one musician (or singer) starts to play (or sing), a second one can join in, in this case, after 4 measures but starting at the beginning. In *The Donkey*, a third musician can also begin after the second player plays 4 measures. All the musicians will be in harmony all the way through and they can repeat the song as many times as they like. *Frére Jacques*, or *Brother John*, is also a round. Rounds are a lot of fun to play as well as to listen to.

The Donkey is a review piece for you in the G Position. There is really nothing new here. The LH plays successive 2nds and 3rds in measures 3 and 4, and then 4ths and 5ths in measures 7 and 8. As you will want to start your practice by playing hands separately, you might start with your LH first which should not give you any problems.

The RH is pretty straight-forward until you get to measure 8. Here, the rhythm in the RH is slightly different than anything you have previously experienced—and it continues right through to the end. It's not really harder, just different.

What makes the RH rhythm a little more complex is beginning the musical phrase on the 4th beat in measures 8, 9 and 10. When you practice on your own, I would like you to count the whole piece right from the beginning. If measures 8–12 give you any difficulty, repeat those measures several times, beginning with the 4th beat of measure 8. When you feel comfortable counting and playing the whole song, play *The Donkey* while singing the words.

If you know another pianist, you can have a lot of fun by having the pianist play the melody part (RH only) one octave higher than your RH part. The pianist does not begin to play until you begin measure 5. You can also sing as you play. For this to work well, you'll both have to keep a steady beat.

THE DONKEY 🔊

G POSITION

Before playing hands together, play LH alone, naming each harmonic interval.

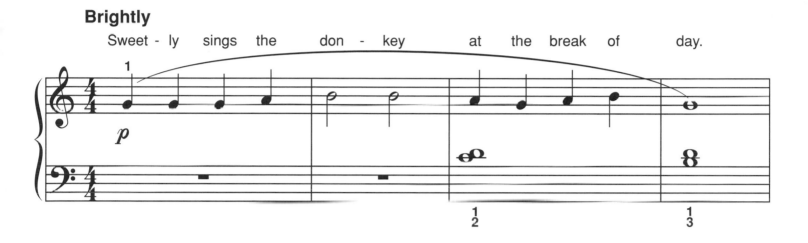

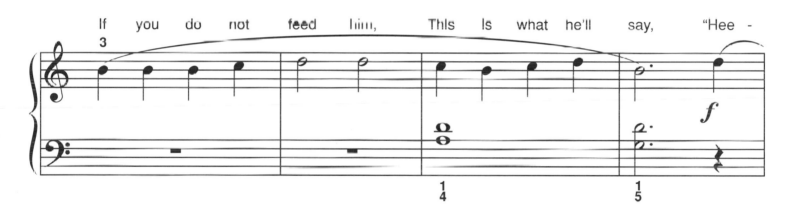

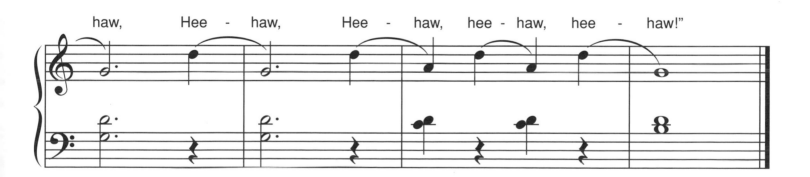

THE DONKEY may be played as a round for two to four pianos.
   The second piano begins after the first has played 4 measures.
   The third begins after the second has played 4 measures, etc.

Play 4 times.

On page 63, you are going to learn something really interesting and also play a song that will bring a smile to your face. I'm sure you've noticed that you haven't played any black keys once you started playing from the music staff. Now you will have your chance.

The Sharp Sign

See the definition of the sharp sign in the upper left hand corner of page 63. When you see this sharp symbol placed before a note, it means to play the next key to the right, whether black or white. For now, the next key to the right will always be a black key. Read the red text at the top of the page explaining that when a sharp appears within a measure, if that note appears again in the same measure, it is also played as a sharped note. However, the following bar line cancels the sharp symbol and if that note appears in the next measure, you will play that note as you always have—in this case, as a white key.

MONEY CAN'T BUY EV'RYTHING

Money Can't Buy Ev'rything is another familiar sounding folk song with a really witty and clever lyric. It suggests that while money can't buy you happiness, it may not be all that bad to have some. This is a fun song to both play *and* sing. Learn this song by first playing the RH alone. There are a few sharps you will be playing but the rhythm is uncomplicated.

The LH is just a series of harmonic 2nds, 3rds and 5ths, all of which you have played before. When you play *Money Can't Buy Ev'rything* with hands together, observe the dynamics (f and p) as you play and be sure to maintain a strict rhythm, as you might expect in a piece that is played in march time. When you feel you can play the song fairly easily, add the lyrics. My students always laugh when they hear me play and sing this song for the very first time.

The Sharp Sign

 The **SHARP SIGN** before a note means play the next key to the RIGHT, whether black or white!

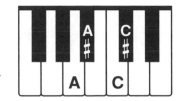

When a SHARP (♯) appears before a note, it applies to that note for the rest of the measure!

Circle the notes that are SHARP:

MONEY CAN'T BUY EV'RYTHING!

March time

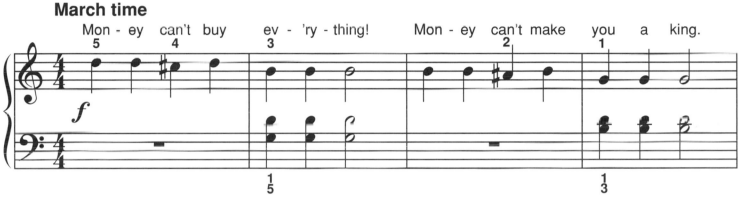

Mon-ey can't buy ev-'ry-thing! Mon-ey can't make you a king.

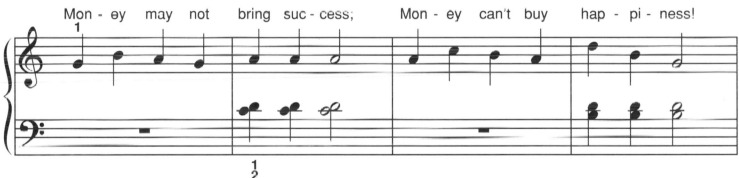

Mon-ey may not bring suc-cess; Mon-ey can't buy hap-pi-ness!

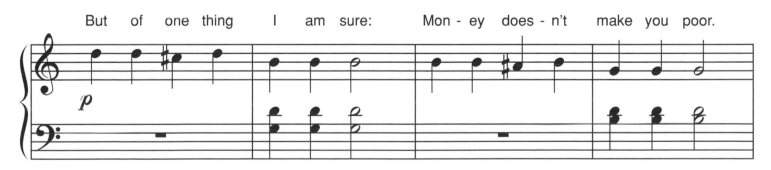

But of one thing I am sure: Mon-ey does-n't make you poor.

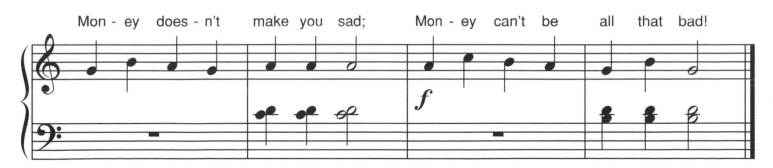

Mon-ey does-n't make you sad; Mon-ey can't be all that bad!

Now that you can play melodies in the G Position, you are going to add two more chords to your repertoire so you can play songs in the G position a little more musically.

The G Major & D7 Chords for Left Hand

Look at the two chord charts at the top of page 65. The G major chord is on the left, the D7 chord is on the right. Sitting at the piano, place your LH on the G chord. Notice that middle C is right between your 1st and 3rd fingers. To play the D7 chord, keep your 1st finger on D, place your 2nd finger on middle C, lift your 3rd finger off B, and stretch your 5th finger down to F♯.

Read the text under the chord charts, and then play the G and D7 chords, alternating back and forth until you can play them easily. There is a short exercise under the text. Notice that all the notes are whole notes and receive 4 counts each. Play this exercise several times, saying the chord names the first time and counting on the repeat.

You now should have no trouble playing the rest of the page. Start with the first full line of music. This is very similar to the short exercise you just played except it is a little longer. Remember to say the chord names the first time and count on the repeat.

The second full line of music contains half and quarter notes so you will be changing chords a little more quickly. Follow the same procedure regarding saying the chord names and counting.

The last or bottom line on this page is a preparation for your next song, *The Cuckoo*. The LH of this piece contains only the G major and D7 chords so you will know half of *The Cuckoo* before you even start.

The G Major & D⁷ Chords for Left Hand

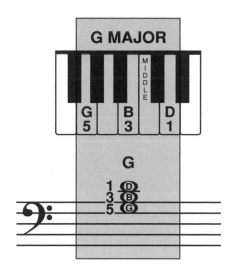

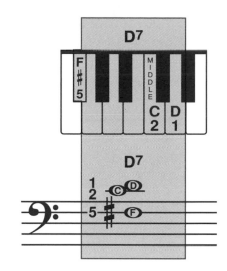

Practice changing from the G chord to the D⁷ chord and back again:

1. 1 plays D in both chords.
2. 2 plays C in the D⁷ chord.
3. Only 5 moves out of G POSITION (down to F♯) for D⁷.

Play the following several times.

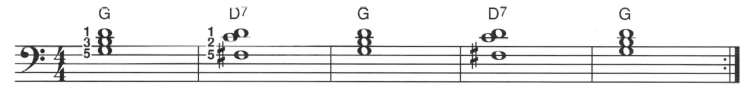

Preparation for *THE CUCKOO:*

THE CUCKOO

You should be able to learn *The Cuckoo* on page 67 fairly quickly. Let's first do a quick scan of the music. Note that this piece is a happy piece and it is also played in $\frac{3}{4}$ time—3 beats or counts to the measure with a quarter note receiving one beat. At the end of the first line, there is a repeat sign.

In line 2, notice the LH D7 chord in measure 5 is tied and held for 2 measures, and so is the G chord in measures 7 and 8. Pay particular attention to the *slur marks*, which indicate *phrases*, in the RH. The notes under and over the *slurs* should be smoothly connected. This will help make *The Cuckoo* sound much more attractive.

Try learning this piece by starting with both hands together. The LH contains only the G and D7 chords, which you now should know very well. If you have any difficulty starting with both hands together, play the RH first, then add the LH.

Play *The Cuckoo* until you know it well. As this is a short piece, try memorizing it and see if you can play it without looking at the music. When you memorize, remember the melody in your head and then play it rather than trying to memorize each individual note.

THE CUCKOO 🔊

Happily

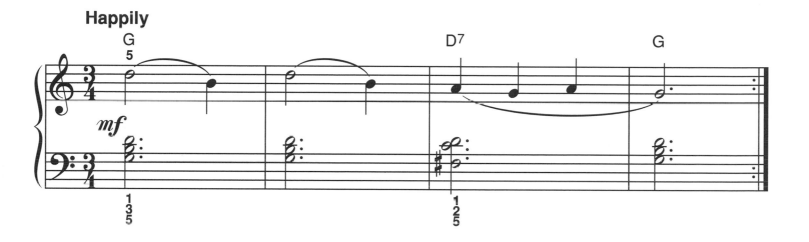

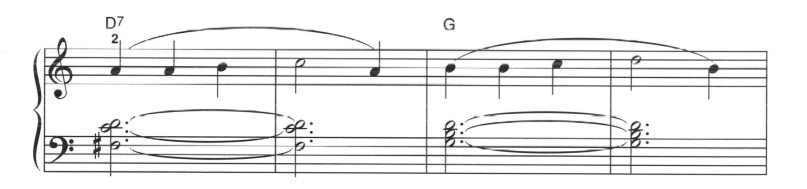

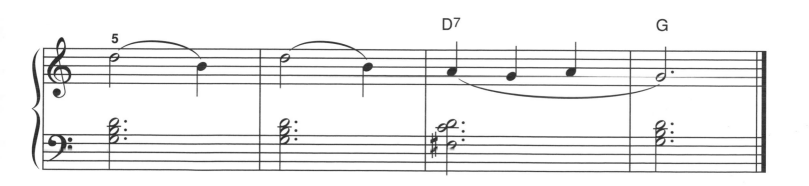

Following the same procedure we have used since the beginning of the book of systematically adding more notes and chords to both the RH and LH, you will now learn how to play the G major and D7 chords with the RH.

The G Major & D7 Chords for Right Hand

The 2 new chords are displayed at the top of page 69 with the G major chord on the left, the D7 chord on the right. Sitting at the piano, look at the chart for the G major chord and place your RH over the keys with your 1st finger on G above middle C, your 3rd finger on B, and your 5th finger on D. As D is the top note of both chords, leave your 5th finger on D for the D7 chord. Now place your 4th finger on C, lift your 3rd finger off B, and stretch your 1st finger down to F♯.

Read the text under the chord charts, and then play the G and D7 chords, alternating back and forth until you can play them easily. There is a short exercise under the text. Notice that all the notes are whole notes and receive 4 counts each. Play this exercise several times, saying the chord names the first time and counting on the repeat. Next, play the long line of music which is very similar to the short exercise. The only difference is that it is longer. As before, say the chords names the first time and count on the repeat.

Block Chords & Broken Chords

When you play all three notes of a chord together, it is called a *block chord*—but there is another way to play chords. When you play the notes of the chord separately, one after the other, you are playing a *broken chord*. The bottom two lines of music demonstrate the difference. Notice that these two lines are in ¾ time.

The upper of the 2 bottom lines shows the G and D7 chords for the RH; the lower line is for the LH. The first G chord on the upper line is a *block chord*, with all 3 notes played together. The next G chord is a *broken chord*. As you can see, the notes of the chord are played one after the other, from the bottom note to the top. The next chord is the D7 *block chord* followed by the D7 *broken chord*.

The lower of the 2 bottom lines shows the G and D7 chords, *block* and *broken*, for the LH. Play the 2 lines, saying the chord names the first time and counting in ¾ time on the repeat. Play these 2 lines until you can play the *block* and *broken* chords smoothly and easily.

The G Major & D⁷ Chords for Right Hand

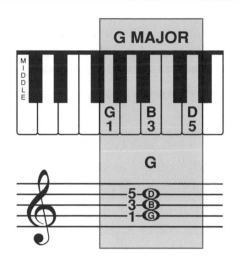
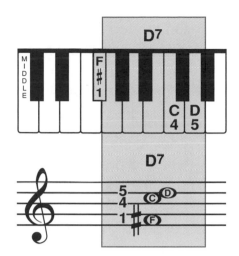

Practice changing from the G chord to the D⁷ chord and back again:

1. 5 plays D in both chords.
2. 4 plays C in the D⁷ chord.
3. Only 1 moves out of G POSITION (down to F♯) for D⁷.

Play several times:

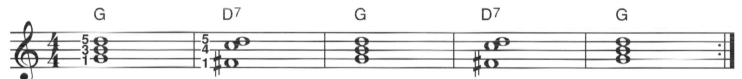

Block Chords & Broken Chords

When all three notes of a chord are played together, it is called a BLOCK chord.
When the three notes of a chord are played separately, it is called a BROKEN chord.

Play several times:

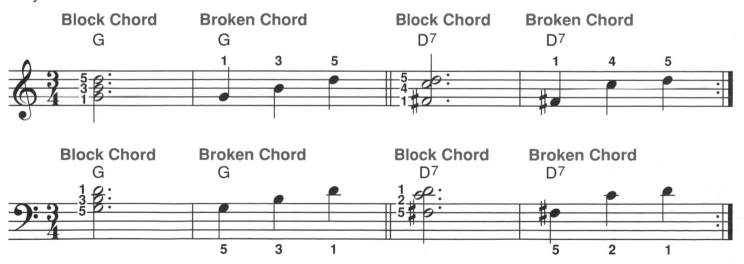

The Damper Pedal

On the top of page 71, you will see a diagram of the 3 pedals at the bottom of the piano. Each pedal has a different function. The one on the right is called the *damper pedal*, and is the one most commonly used. When you hold this pedal down, the sound will continue after you release the key while holding the pedal down. Read the text in the pink box.

Look at the *pedal sign*, located on your page under the pink box. This symbol indicates when to press the pedal down, how long to hold it down, and when to raise it up to stop the sound. Sitting at the piano, press down the *damper pedal* with your right foot several times to get the feel of it. When you play a piece that includes *pedal marks*, keep your right foot over the *damper pedal* so you will be in position to press it down and raise it when indicated in the music.

HARP SONG

The *Harp Song* involves playing broken chords while using the pedal, up and down, throughout the piece. A harpist often plays broken chords and this piece was written in that style. It is important to raise the pedal as you play the RH D in measure 4 and then to press it down right *after* you have played the LH F♯ in the second line. If you press the pedal down too soon, you might retain the sound of the D, the last RH note of the first line.

Visually scan the music and see what you can learn before you begin to play. Look at the tempo marking first—you are to play the piece *moderately slow*. Then look at the time signature—the *Harp Song* is in ¾ time. Notice the 2 dynamic signs under the treble time signature, *mf* and *p*. Play me*zzo forte* (*moderately loud*) the first time and *piano* (*soft*) on the repeat.

Do you see the chord symbols above the treble staff? You can see that the first line of music contains just the G chord; the second line, just the D7 chord; the third line, just the G chord; and the bottom line, the D7 chord for the first two measures and the G chord for the last two. When you analyze a piece first, it becomes much easier and quicker for you to learn.

After you have learned to play this piece smoothly, with the pedal being held down and raised appropriately, you can have some fun and make this piece sound more like a harp while giving you a chance to look and sound like a concert pianist.

Read the text at the bottom of the page. **Option 1** is to play measures 1 and 2 as written and measures 3 and 4 one octave higher. You will then continue to play in this style for the rest of the piece. **Option 2** is to play measures 1 and 2 an octave lower and measures 3 and 4 as written. You will then continue to play in this style for the rest of the piece. With these 2 options, you will soon feel like you are performing like a concert artist.

The Damper Pedal

- Use the RIGHT foot on the damper pedal.

- Always keep your heel on the floor.

- Use your ankle like a hinge.

The RIGHT pedal is called the **DAMPER** pedal.

When you hold the damper pedal down, any tone you sound will continue after you release the key.

This sign means:

PEDAL DOWN   PEDAL UP

HOLD PEDAL

HARP SONG 🔊 25

Many pieces are made entirely of broken chords, as this one is!

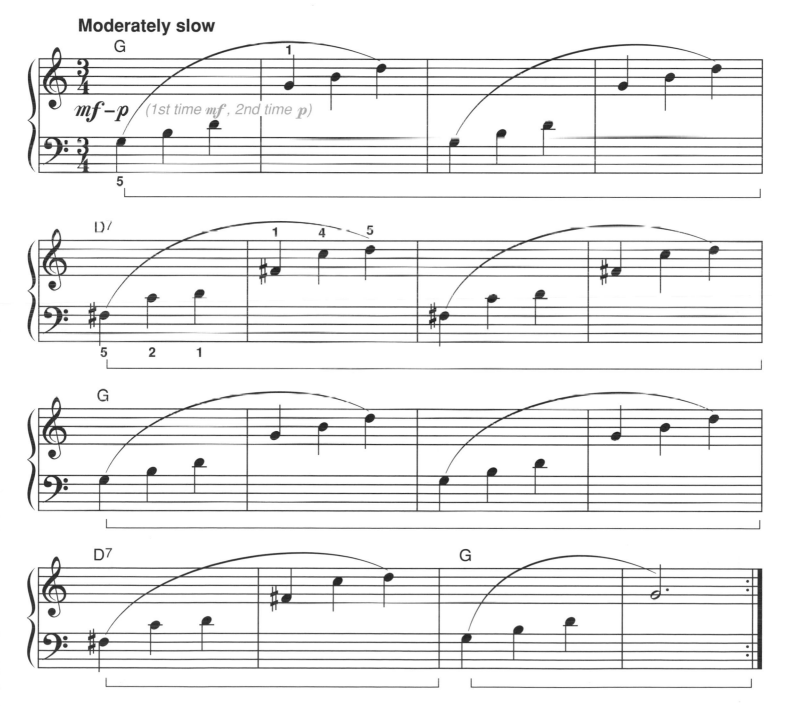

Also play *HARP SONG* in the following ways:

1. Play the third and fourth measures of each line one octave higher than written.
2. Play the first and second measures of each line one octave lower than written.

Now that you have become familiar with the 5-note G position, you are going to expand the range of this position to 6 notes, 1st with the LH, then with the RH.

Introducing (E) for Left Hand

Look at the top of page 73 where you will see E highlighted above the bass staff. The note is placed on the second ledger line above the staff and is the E located just to the right of middle C. Sitting at the piano, look at the keyboard chart below the staff and place your LH on the G position as shown, with your 1st finger on D. Now move your 1st finger one white key higher to E, then back to D, making sure you move only your finger and not your whole hand. Move your 1st finger back and forth between D and E several times.

The first line of music under the keyboard chart is a series of broken chords. Play the first line several times, following the directions for fingering below the staff. The notes in the first measure form the G major broken chord. Say the notes of this exercise the first time: G-B-D, G-C-E, G-B-D, G-C-E, counting in $\frac{3}{4}$ time on the repeat. Repeat this exercise several times.

A New Position of the C major Chord

You already have played the G major and C major chords. If I tried to play the chords one after the other as you have learned them, it would be clumsy to do and would not sound very smooth.

Here is an interesting thing about chords. When you play the 3 notes of a C chord, C is the lowest note, followed by E and G. When you play these 3 notes in any order, E-G-C or G-C-E, you still have a C major chord. When you are playing in G position, it is more convenient to play the C chord as G-C-E with G as the lowest note, rather than C-E-G, the way you've previously played the chord.

Read the text under *A New Position of the C Major Chord*. It explains how much easier it is to play the G chord followed by this new position of the C chord. The left pink box highlights the G major chord, which you originally learned on page 65. To play the G major chord and then move easily to the new C major chord, place your LH over the G major chord. The 5th finger is the bottom note of both chords. While holding G down with your 5th finger, raise your 3rd finger off B and place your 2nd finger on C. Finally, raise your 1st finger off D and move it up to E—and that's the new C major chord. This new position is shown in the right pink box.

Read the text below the pink keyboard charts and then play the bottom line of music several times, saying the chord names the first time and counting on the repeat. Try to play the chord changes smoothly.

Introducing Ⓔ for Left Hand

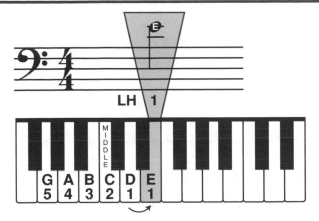

TO FIND E:

Place the LH in **G POSITION.**
Reach finger 1 one white key to the right!

Play slowly. Say the note names as you play.

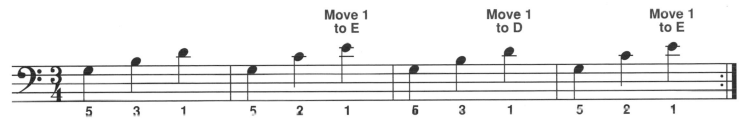

A New Position of the C Major Chord

You have already played the C MAJOR CHORD with C as the lowest note. **C E G.**

When you play these same three notes in any order, you still have a C MAJOR CHORD.
When you are playing in G POSITION, it is most convenient to play G as the lowest note: **G C E.**

The following diagrams show how easy it is to move from the G MAJOR CHORD to the
C MAJOR CHORD, when G is the lowest note of both chords.

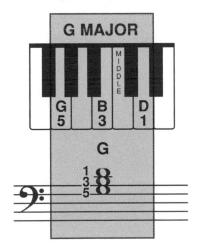

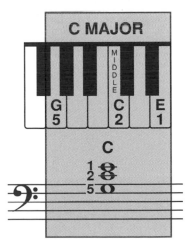

Practice changing from the G chord to the C chord and back again:

1. 5 plays G in both chords.
2. 2 plays C in the C chord.
3. Only 1 moves out of G POSITION (up to E) for the C chord.

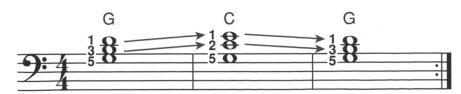

Warm-Up using G, D7 & C Chords

The warm-up at the top of page 75 introduces a new way of playing broken chords. You can play a G broken chord another way than just single notes played one after the other. You can play the bottom note first, then add harmonic intervals on the next beat or beats.

Look at the top line of music, which is in $\frac{3}{4}$ time. Play the G major chord in the 1st measure. The 2nd measure includes the new version of the broken chord with G played on the 1st count and the harmonic interval B-D on the 2nd and 3rd counts. As the G is a quarter note, lift off it when playing the harmonic intervals.

The 3rd measure is the new position of the C chord, while the 4th measure is the new version of the broken chord. The 5th measure is the D7 chord followed by its new broken chord version. The exercise ends with the broken G chord and a final G. Say the chord names the first time, saying *G-bro-ken* for the broken chords, and counting on the repeat.

BEAUTIFUL BROWN EYES

You've probably heard *Beautiful Brown Eyes* many times. Scanning the music you can see the song is in $\frac{3}{4}$ time, is played moderately fast, has chord symbols placed above the music, and includes pedal signs.

Notice also there are LH tied chords in the first 2 measures of each line and broken chords in the last 2 measures of each line.

Start by playing the LH alone, then play the RH alone, and finally, play with hands together. Remember the dynamic sign is *mezzo forte*, *moderately loud*, and there are pedal markings in the last two measures of every line. To make *Beautiful Brown Eyes* sound beautiful, try to play the long slurs smoothly connected. This should be a fun song for you to play.

Warn-Up using G, D⁷ & C Chords

This warm-up introduces a new way of playing BROKEN CHORDS.

BEAUTIFUL BROWN EYES 🔊

Moderately fast

What you did for the LH on pages 73 and 75, you will now do for the RH on pages 77 and 79. Because of the way this course is logically sequenced and presented, the learning process becomes easier and quicker than in other courses. Let's see how quickly we can now get through this page. One problem, though—adults seem to intellectually understand more quickly than younger students but it may take them a bit longer to have their fingers do what their mind tells them. You already know a lot about this page from the previous lesson so the secret to success is to practice a little more. There is an old story you've probably heard. Two tourists visiting New York City ask a policeman how to get to Carnegie Hall. His answer was simply, "Practice, practice, practice."

Introducing E for Right Hand

Look at the top of the page 77 where you will see E highlighted in the top space of the treble staff. The note is one note higher than D, the top note of the G position. Sitting at the piano, look at the keyboard chart below the staff and place your RH over the notes G–D with your 1st finger on G. Now shift fingers 2, 3, 4 and 5 one white key to the right ending with finger 2 on B, finger 3 on C, finger 4 on D, and finger 5 on A. Then shift those fingers back to the G position again.

The first line of music is played as broken chords, just as on page 73. Play the first line of music several times, following the directions for fingering above the staff. The notes in the 1st measure form the G major broken chord. Say the notes of this exercise the first time: G-B-D, G-C-E, G-B-D, G-C-E, counting in $\frac{3}{4}$ time on the repeat. Repeat this exercise several times.

New C Major Chord Position—Right Hand

You already have played the G major (G-B-D) and C major (C-E-G) chords. In this new version of the RH C chord, the bottom note G is played by the 1st finger and is the same for both chords. After playing the G major chord, shift your 3rd and 5th fingers one key to the right, on to C and E. You will now be playing G-C-E. Go back and forth between both chords several times.

The bottom line of music on the page is a short exercise in playing these two chords. Try to smoothly connect the chords as you play. Read the text at the bottom of the page and play the bottom line of music several times.

Introducing (E) for Right Hand

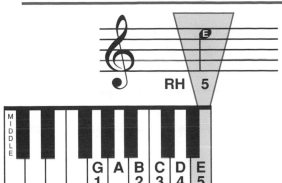

TO FIND E:

Place the RH in **G POSITION.**
Leave finger 1 on G.
Shift all other fingers one white key to the right.

Play slowly. Say the note names as you play.

New C Major Chord Position—Right Hand

Notice that *two* fingers must move to the right when changing from the G MAJOR CHORD to the C MAJOR CHORD.

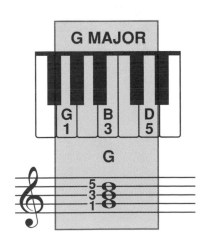

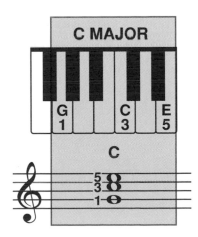

Practice changing from the G chord to the C chord and back again:

1. 1 plays G in both chords.
2. 3 moves up to C and 5 moves up to E for the C chord.

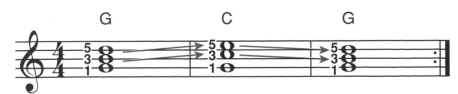

Warm-Up using G, D7 & C Chords

The top exercise on page 79 is somewhat similar to the bottom line of music on page 77 except you will be adding the D7 chord (see page 69) and you will be playing in $\frac{3}{4}$ time with a chord played on each beat. On page 77, each chord was made up of whole notes and received 4 beats. As you will now be playing the chords more quickly, start slowly and gradually increase your speed.

ALPINE MELODY

The LH of *Alpine Melody* may remind you of a Swiss yodeling song. The melody is in the LH, with the accompaniment chords in the RH. Because the melody is in the LH, to sound good play the LH slightly louder than the RH. This melody will actually sound a little Swiss when you play it smoothly.

Notice the new bass note E on the third line of music, 2nd measure. Also observe the slurs and smoothly connect the melody notes underneath them. The RH is a little trickier when played alone but fits easily when played together with the LH. Start your practice by playing the LH alone, then adding the RH.

Notice that you are in $\frac{3}{4}$ time, and you will be playing moderately slow and *piano,* that is, *softly.* There are pedal markings under the first, second, and fourth lines of music. Also notice the chord symbols over the music which will alert you to the chord changes. Very importantly, look at the very last measure at the bottom of the page—it tells you to repeat the entire piece with both hands played one octave higher.

Before you begin, point to all of these music symbols on the page with one of your hands. This is always good practice before starting a new piece. By doing this, you will not be surprised as you play.

So lower your thermostat and imagine you are in the Swiss Alps. When you can play *Alpine Melody* smoothly, have a hot chocolate and you'll almost believe you are there.

Warm-Up using G, D⁷ & C Chords

Play SLOWLY at first, then gradually increase speed.

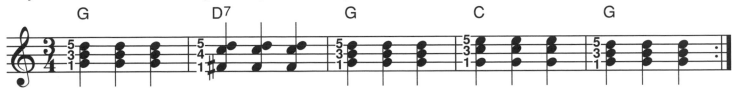

ALPINE MELODY

The LH melody of this piece consists entirely of BROKEN CHORDS,
which are the same as the BLOCK CHORDS played by the RH in each measure!

*Play both hands 8va
(one octave higher)
the 2nd time!*

One of the wonderful things about playing the piano and learning about music is that you can constantly learn new things that are not necessarily harder. If you remember the song *Everything Old is New Again* by Peter Allen, you'll know what I mean. On page 81, we are going to take something you already know and learn to do it in a new way.

Middle C Position

Look at the keyboard chart and music staff on the top right of page 81 and you will see a new hand position, the Middle C Position. In this position, the RH plays notes C up to G with fingers 1 to 5, just as in the C Position.

The LH in Middle C Position also begins with finger 1 on Middle C and plays the notes C down to F with fingers 1 to 5. By placing the 1st finger of both hands on Middle C, each hand will be in the Middle C Position. As you can see, the 1st fingers of each hand will overlap, but as you only need one finger to play a key, you will play middle C with either your RH or LH. The music on the staff will guide you.

Look at the two exercises in the middle of the page. The bass staff on the left is in the Middle C LH position. Place your LH in the Middle C Position and play and say the note names several times until the LH notes become very familiar to you. After this, play and say the notes names in the treble staff on the right—then play the RH but as you already know this, just do it a few times as a review.

THUMBS ON C!

Thumbs on C! is an exercise type of piece with the LH playing the first line of music and the RH playing the second. Let's take a quick survey of the printed music. The tempo is *moderately slow*, the dynamic sign is m*ezzo forte*, or *moderately loud*. The piece is in $\frac{4}{4}$ time and if you look at the very last measure on the second line, you will see a repeat sign so you will be playing this piece twice. When you play *Thumbs on C*, say the note names the first time and count on the repeat. Do this several times until you have no trouble reading the LH notes.

Middle C Position

The MIDDLE C POSITION uses notes you already know!

- RH is in C POSITION.
- LH moves one note down from G POSITION.
- Both thumbs are now on Middle C.

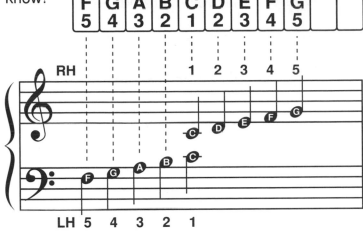

Play and say the note names. Do this several times!

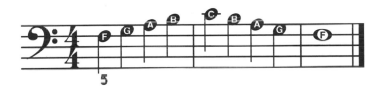

Thumbs on C!

Moderately slow

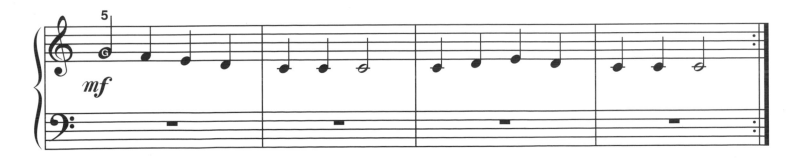

New Dynamic Signs

At the top of page 83 in the pink box, you will see 2 new dynamic signs. Until now, you have played all the exercises and pieces either *piano, mezzo forte* or *forte*. These, however, are not our only options when playing the piano.

Crescendo and *diminuendo* are hairpin-like signs that tell you to play the music *gradually louder* or *gradually softer*. It allows you to be more expressive at the piano. *Crescendo* means to play gradually louder, *diminuendo* (think of the word *diminish*) means to play gradually softer.

Starting softly *(piano)* on middle C with your RH 3rd finger, play C repeatedly and gradually *increase* the volume until you reach *forte*—that would be a *crescendo*. Now do the opposite, starting loudly *(forte)* with your LH 3rd finger, play middle C repeatedly and gradually *decrease* the volume until you reach *piano*—that would be a *diminuendo.*

WALTZ TIME

The piece on this page is titled *Waltz Time*, and it allows you to play a *diminuendo* and a *crescendo* for the first time. Like *Alpine Melody* on page 79, the melody is in the LH so you will play the LH slightly louder than the RH.

In the 6th measure (second line), the *crescendo* (gradually louder) starts on bass G with the LH. As the starting dynamic sign is *piano*, start the LH *crescendo* playing softly, then gradually increase the volume to about *mezzo-forte* until you reach the LH C in the next measure. Try playing those bass notes several times, gradually increasing the volume as you play.

In the 7th measure, 2nd beat, the *diminuendo* (gradually softer) begins on E-G with the RH. Start the *diminuendo* playing *mezzo forte*, then gradually decrease the volume to *piano* until you play LH G in the 8th measure (last measure of the second line). Play measures 6 through 8 with both hands several times until you can perform the *crescendo* and *diminuendo* smoothly. These 3 measures appear again at the end of the piece.

Let's take a quick survey of the music. *Waltz Time* is played at a moderate waltz tempo. The word *tempo* means *the rate of speed* at which you play. As waltzes are always played in $\frac{3}{4}$ time, this piece has a time signature of $\frac{3}{4}$ time. *Piano* is the starting dynamic sign. As you look through each line, you will see your first *crescendo* mark in the second line, followed by a *diminuendo* sign in the next measure. This happens again in the last line. And finally, there is a repeat sign at the end of the last line. Play both hands an octave higher on the repeat. Count aloud the first few times you play *Waltz Time.*

WALTZ TIME 🔊

NEW DYNAMIC SIGNS

Crescendo (gradually louder)   *Diminuendo* (gradually softer)

CONTINUE TO READ BY PATTERNS! For LH, think:

"C, same, down a 2nd, down a 2nd, up a 2nd," etc.

Moderate waltz tempo (tempo = speed)

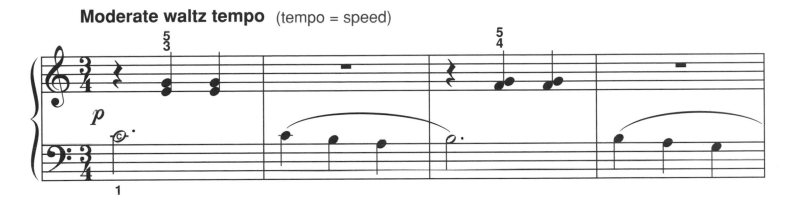

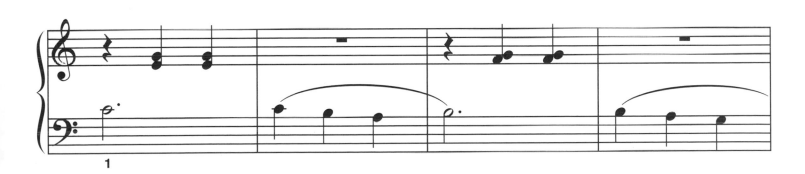

*Repeat with both hands 8va
(one octave higher).*

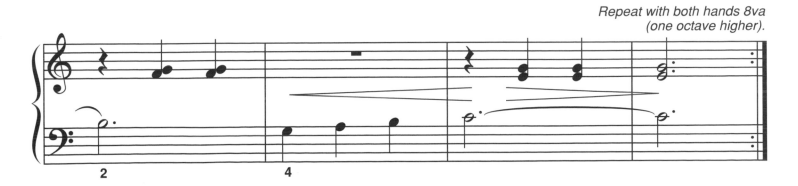

The next 4 pages of the course probably represent the most dramatic growth in your ability to play the piano since you began. These pages will introduce you to something new—*eighth notes*—but first things first.

Fermata Sign

At the top of page 85 in the pink box, the *fermata* sign is introduced. It tells you to hold the note, or rest, longer than its value. How long? Well that's up to you and where your own musical judgment comes in. Generally speaking, about half again as long as the note or rest value. That's not a rule, just a guide.

GOOD MORNING TO YOU!

Good Morning to You is a familiar song to children and is frequently used by students to welcome their teacher. Look at the beginning of the bottom line of music and you will see a line under the music where "teacher" would be sung but we've made a change so you can insert any name you prefer. Notice the song begins with an incomplete measure with the missing 2 beats found in the last measure.

Also note the song is in the new Middle C Position, it's to be played happily in $\frac{3}{4}$ time, and the dynamic sign is *mezzo forte*. As you play, the melody will begin to switch back and forth from the LH to the RH in the 1st measure of the second line, and then through the rest of the piece. Just play the melody notes a little louder than the accompaniment. It requires you to concentrate a little more as you play, but that's something you should always be doing. In the 1st measure of the bottom line, there are 2 *fermata* signs on the 2nd beat—pause there a little longer. There are also 2 *fermata* signs in the last measure.

Start slowly and gradually build up your speed. When you can play *Good Morning to You* easily, get ready to be the star of every birthday party that has a piano in the house.

This sign is called a **FERMATA.**

Hold the note under the fermata *longer* than its value.

GOOD MORNING TO YOU!

MIDDLE C POSITION

Happily

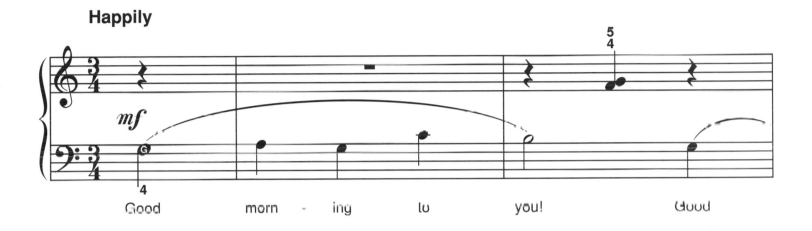

Good morn - ing to you! Good

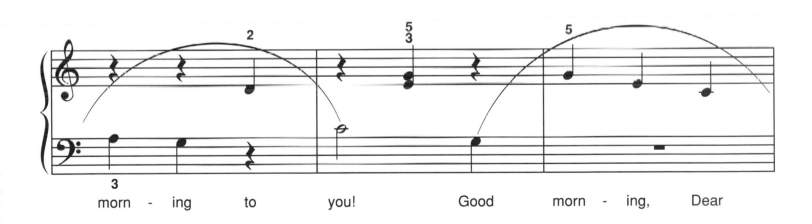

morn - ing to you! Good morn - ing, Dear

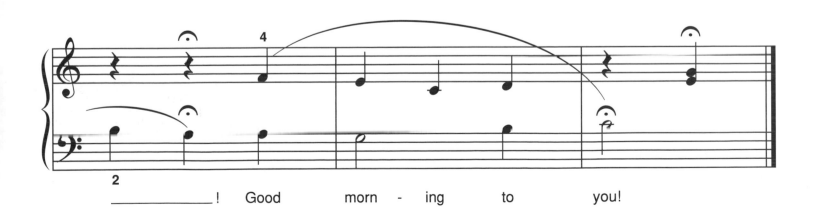

_____ ! Good morn - ing to you!

Self-Teaching Study Guide

Eighth Notes

In the pink box at the top of page 87, you will see a pair of *eighth notes.* Eighth notes may sound complex but trust me, they are not. They are played twice as fast as quarter notes and when you can play eighth notes easily, you will be able to play many more songs than you have been able to play so far.

The text at the top of the page explains that when 8th notes are in a piece, it is better to count "1 &, 2 &, 3 &" rather than "1, 2, 3." In this way you can split each count in half. Look at the notes on the long, single line just below the text. Clap or tap these notes while counting aloud. Count with "and" (&): 1 &, 2 &, 3 &.

HAPPY BIRTHDAY TO YOU!

Happy Birthday to You is identical to *Good Morning to You* except, and this is very important, it contains 8th notes. You should have almost no trouble playing *Happy Birthday to You* the first or second time you play it. You must count this as 1 &, 2 &, 3 &, if you are to perform the 8th notes successfully. Because the song begins with an incomplete measure, start your count with 1 &, 2 &, and begin to play the 8th notes on 3 &. Get ready to be the life of future birthday parties!

Before we end this lesson, I'd like to give you some good news. With the completion of this lesson you can play a lot more music than you might think. For example, the publishers of this book, Alfred Publishing Co., has available a number of other books that are coordinated with the book you are now using. We have a very popular book, the *Adult Christmas Book,* Level 1 (#2466), that allows you to play some of your favorite Christmas carols. And for those of you more interested in sacred music, we have the *Adult Sacred Book,* Level 1 (#2468) that many pianists enjoy.

There are two books that include popular songs, *Greatest Hits* (#16505) and *Christmas Hits* (#17108) in Alfred's Basic Adult Piano Course that you can also begin now. The songs are sequenced the same as this book in grade level, though the page references in those books will be different. There are also many other books of popular music in Alfred's *Big Note* series that you can play now. Ask your music dealer about these books and select one or two that have songs you would like to play.

Eighth Notes

Two eighth notes are played in the time of **one quarter note.**

When a piece contains eighth notes, count:

"**1—&**" or "**quar—ter**"   for each quarter note;
"**1—&**" or "**two eighths**"   for each pair of eighth notes.

Eighth notes are usually played in **pairs.**

COUNT: "1   &"
or: "two eighths"

Clap (or tap) these notes, counting aloud:

HAPPY BIRTHDAY TO YOU! 🔊

HAPPY BIRTHDAY is exactly the same as *GOOD MORNING TO YOU,* except for the eighth notes!

One of the attractive features of learning to play is the various styles of music you can perform on the piano. Each style has its own characteristic and unique appeal. As an example, you can play the *blues*, you can play *jazz,* and you can play *ragtime*—and you will be playing some of these styles by the end of the course. *Sacred* music is another style of music and it has played an important role in church services for a long time. One form of sacred music that is frequently sung is the *spiritual*. The music is of American origin and is usually a simple melody with elements of folk, gospel and occasionally jazz.

STANDING IN THE NEED OF PRAYER

Standing in the Need of Prayer on page 89 is a spiritual that is fun to play. You know almost everything on this page. However, what you don't know is under the last measure of the music: the text in red, *D. C. al Fine,* an abbreviation for *Da Capo al Fine* (pronounced *Feé-nay*).

It means that when you reach the end of this line of music, you go back to the beginning and, without missing a beat, play the music again until you see the word *Fine,* which means *end* in Italian. You will see *Fine* under the music at the end of the second line. The last measure only has 3 beats and where do you think the missing beat is? If you said the 1st incomplete measure, you would be correct but the beginning of the third line also includes an incomplete measure. This will be the longest piece you've played so far. Notice we are back in the C Position. I think you will enjoy both playing and singing this spiritual.

There really isn't any good reason why you can't begin to play this piece right now. Scan the music and make note of the tempo marking (not too fast), the time signature ($\frac{4}{4}$ time), the dynamic signs (there are 2 *crescendo* and 2 *diminuendo* signs), the incomplete measures, and finally, slurs and chords in the LH. It's got everything. The LH contains the C, G7 and F chords. You might want to start playing the LH first and then add the RH.

To review these 3 chords, turn back to page 51 and play the Warm-Up exercise at the top of the page a few times. Some students write the names of the chords in light pencil right under the notes as an aid to learning, but it is better if you recognize the chords by just reading the music.

STANDING IN THE NEED OF PRAYER 🔊

For this popular spiritual, we return to C POSITION (LH 5 on C).

Rhythmically, not too fast

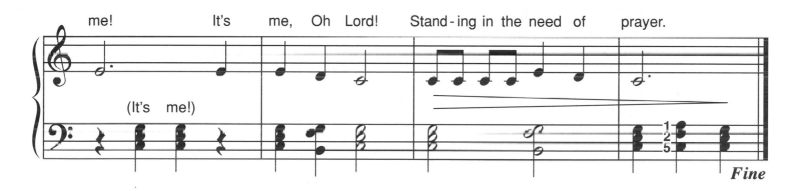

D. C. al Fine (Da Capo al Fine) means repeat from the beginning and play to the end *(Fine)*.

THE GIFT TO BE SIMPLE

On page 91, we will be playing an old Shaker melody that Aaron Copland used in his well-known orchestral suite, *Appalachian Spring*. It is called *The Gift to Be Simple* and the melody is as beautiful as it is simple.

For the first time, the LH will be playing in 2 positions within one piece, the middle C and C Positions. Because you have not played in two positions before, let's take a look at the LH and see how it is done. Under the first complete measure, you will see directions in red that says, "Move LH to C Position." By moving your LH during the rests, you will have no trouble playing the C chord in the second complete measure. The same hand movement occurs in the 5th and 6th measures (third line).

There is one more position change for the LH and that occurs in the second line. Move your LH in the 2nd measure of line 2 while the RH is playing, to prepare to play the B on the count of 2&. It's an easy move if you prepare in advance.

As moving the LH is new, I would like you to start your practice by playing the LH alone. Concentrate on measures 1 and 2 and then 3 and 4. As measures 5 and 6 are the same as 1 and 2, the only thing new for you is contained in the first 2 lines. Because the tempo of the piece is moderately slow, it should not cause you any great difficulty.

Something new occurs when you get to the 1st measure of the last line when playing the repeat. Notice the *ritardando* sign—it means to gradually slow down for the ending. Also, the *diminuendo* in the last measure means to gradually get softer and because of the *fermatas*, hold the last notes a little longer than one beat.

THE GIFT TO BE SIMPLE 🔊

COMBINING MIDDLE C POSITION & C POSITION

You are now ready to play music that involves more than one position. This piece begins with the hands in MIDDLE C POSITION. After the first full measure is played, the LH moves to C POSITION to play chords. Change positions as indicated in the music.

This beautiful old Shaker melody was used by the famous American composer, Aaron Copland, in his well-known symphonic composition, *Appalachian Spring.*

ritardando means *gradually slowing.*

You are now going to learn to play a new kind of note. It is called a *dotted quarter note* and it allows you to perform songs that contain an easy and appealing rhythm.

Introducing Dotted Quarter Notes

Page 93 is titled *Introducing Dotted Quarter Notes*. When we introduced the dotted half note we mentioned that the purpose of the dot is to increase the value of the note by one-half of its original value.

Look at the top pink box which explains that a *dotted half note* is equal to a *half note* tied to a *quarter note*. Look to the right of the box and you will see the music written out. As half of 2 counts is 1, that explains how a half note receives 2 counts, and a dotted half note, which increases the value of the half note by half, receives 3 counts.

Look at the lower red box and you will see a similar explanation for a *dotted quarter note*, which is a *quarter note* tied to an *8th note*. As the dot increases the original value of the note by one-half, a quarter note receives 1 count and a dotted quarter note receives 1 1/2 counts. This is a situation where demonstrating the dotted quarter note may be easier than explaining it.

As the first line of music half way down the page includes a repeat sign, clap and count the line twice. This line demonstrates the rhythm of a quarter note tied to an 8th note. You should count 1 &, 2 &, 3 &, 4 &, as you clap the notes in the correct rhythm.

Look at the bottom line of music. Compare it to the line above it. They are written differently but they will sound the same. This time, instead of clapping, play middle C in the correct rhythm while counting. Play this bottom line several times until it feels natural.

Introducing Dotted Quarter Notes

A DOT INCREASES THE LENGTH OF A NOTE BY ONE HALF ITS VALUE.

| **A dotted half note** is equal to a half note tied to a quarter note. |

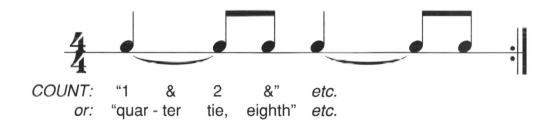

| **A dotted quarter note** is equal to a quarter note tied to an eighth note. |

Clap (or tap) the following rhythm. Clap **ONCE** for each note, counting aloud.

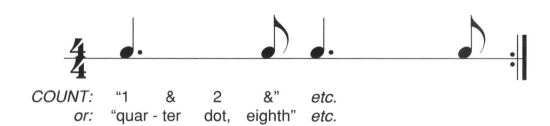

The only difference between the following measure and the one directly above it is the way they are written. They are played the same.

In $\frac{4}{4}$ or $\frac{3}{4}$ time, the DOTTED QUARTER NOTE is almost *always* followed by an EIGHTH NOTE!

Measures from Familiar Songs Using Dotted Quarter Notes

Page 95 is titled, *Measures from Familiar Songs Using Dotted Quarter Notes*. Play and count the first line, which is *Silent Night*, 3 ways: first, count and clap the notes; second, play and count; and finally, play and sing the words. Knowing how *Silent Night* sounds should help you to play the dotted quarter and 8th notes in the correct rhythm.

Practice each of the music lines below on this page in the same manner. The second line of music includes a few measures from *Deck the Halls*. When you play this line, include the repeat. There are two sets of lyrics, numbered 1. and 2.—sing 1 the first time and 2 on the repeat.

The next line of music is *Auld Lang Syne*, which, as you know, is sung mostly on New Year's Eve. Notice it starts with an incomplete measure.

The bottom line of music is the famous wedding song, *Here Comes the Bride.* By now, you should be having no trouble with dotted quarter notes followed by 8th notes. When you complete *Here Comes the Bride*, sing and play your way through this entire page, starting at the top. There is more music coming with this rhythm so it is important to play it smoothly and easily.

Measures from Familiar Songs Using Dotted Quarter Notes

1. Count & clap (or tap) the notes.   2. Play & count.   3. Play & sing the words.

C POSITION

Si - lent night,   Ho - ly night,

MIDDLE C POSITION (Both thumbs on Middle C)

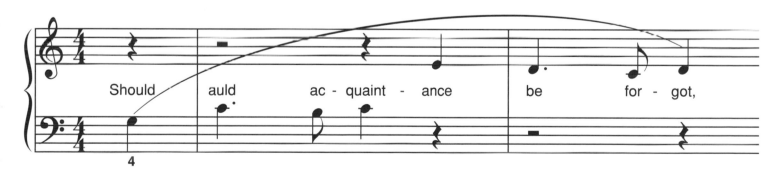

1. Deck the halls with boughs of hol - ly,
2. 'Tis the sea - son to be jol - ly,
Fa - la - la - la - la - la - la - la - la - la!

MIDDLE C POSITION

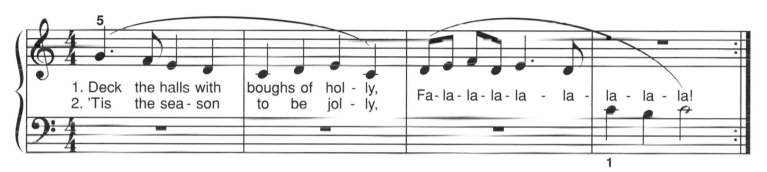

Should auld ac - quaint - ance be for - got,

C POSITION

Here comes the bride!   All dressed in white!

Self-Teaching Study Guide

ALOUETTE

Your new piece on page 97 is titled *Alouette*, a popular French folk song. When you learn to play it, I think you'll find the music familiar. *Alouette* is in C Position, is played brightly, and starts *forte*.

Alouette uses 2 chords in the LH, the C and G7 chords. You can use the chord symbols as a guide but you should be able to read the chords right from the music. If you know someone who plays guitar, they can use these chord symbols to strum along with you as you play and it will add a nice accompaniment to your performance.

The RH melody consists of 4 measures that include the new dotted quarter note in measures 1 and 3. They appear again identically in measures 9 and 11. When you learn the first 4 measures, you've also learned measures 9 to 12. When you begin to play *Alouette*, first practice measures 1–4 several times before playing the rest of the piece.

Trace your finger along the first line and you'll notice a *piano* dynamic sign in the 3rd measure. There are *crescendo* and *diminuendo* signs in the second line. The third line begins with *forte,* and the fourth line contains a *piano* sign. I'd like you to concentrate on the dynamics as you play. Playing louder and softer adds to the musicality of the piece and it just makes it sound so much better. Finally, look for the slurs and smoothly connect the notes in measures 1, 2, 3 and 4, and then again in measures 9, 10, 11 and 12. When you begin to play *Alouette*, play hands separately at first. It's a simple melody and I think you'll learn it quickly.

ALOUETTE  34 🔊))

C POSITION

Brightly

French folk song

Measuring 6ths

Page 99 is titled *Measuring 6ths*. You've already played a span of a 6th in the G7 and D7 chords. Now you will learn to play them both as melodic and harmonic intervals. To play a 6th, you skip 4 white keys on the keyboard. On the staff, they are written from line-to-space or from space-to-line. See the diagram at the top center of the page and you will see an interval of a 6th on the keyboard without the black keys. See the pink box to the right to see how a 6th looks on the staff (line note to space note and vice versa).

Look at the keyboard chart at the top left of the page. When you start to play, place your fingers in the RH C Position. The 6th interval is the C Position plus one note, the A. While holding treble C down with your 1st finger, lift fingers 2, 3 and 4 off the keyboard, and play A with your 5th finger. That is an interval of a 6th.

Play the *melodic intervals* on the first line of music several times, saying the intervals as you play. After playing this exercise several times, play the *harmonic intervals* on the second line (both notes played together), saying the intervals as you play. Re-read the text at the top of the page, then play lines 1 and 2 again, saying the intervals one more time as you play each line twice. Only the 6th is new but by repeating these exercises, you will have a strong foundation of intervals in the C Position.

You will now follow the same procedure with LH 6ths. Look at the keyboard chart in the bottom half of the page and place your fingers in the LH C Position. While holding bass C down with your 5th finger, lift fingers 2, 3 and 4 off the keyboard, and play A with your 1st finger. That is an interval of a 6th. It's probably a little easier moving your 1st finger up one key with your LH than it was to move your RH 5th finger up one key to A. The thumbs spread much more easily than any of the other fingers.

Play the *melodic intervals* on the third line of music on the lower half of the page several times, saying the intervals as you play. After playing this exercise several times, play the *harmonic intervals* in the bottom line, both notes played together, saying the intervals as you play. Also play this line several times. There is not much new here and you should be able to play through the entire page rather quickly.

Measuring 6ths

When you skip 4 white keys, the interval is a **6th**.

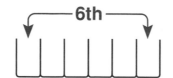

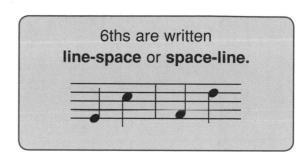

6ths are written
line-space or **space-line**.

RH

This is C POSITION plus 1 note (A) played with 5.

RH 5 plays G or A!

Say the names of these intervals as you play!

MELODIC INTERVALS

HARMONIC INTERVALS

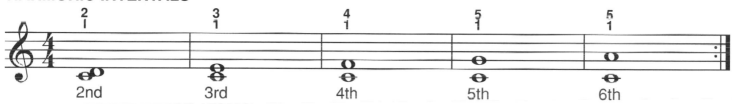

LH

This is C POSITION plus 1 note (A) played with 1.

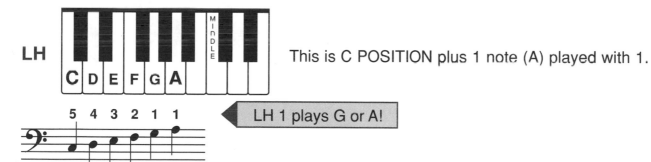

LH 1 plays G or A!

Say the names of these intervals as you play!

MELODIC INTERVALS

HARMONIC INTERVALS

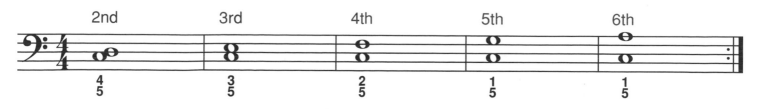

By knowing how to play melodic and harmonic 6ths, your ability to perform more songs increases dramatically as most songs include intervals larger than a 5th. As you learn not only larger intervals but other musical terms as well, more and more appealing songs become available to you.

LAVENDER'S BLUE

Lavender's Blue on page 101 is a familiar folk song. You might have sung it in elementary school. At the top of the page, there is a 2-measure exercise consisting of harmonic 5ths and 6ths for both hands. You should begin here. Play the LH exercise several times, then play the RH exercise several times, saying the harmonic intervals as you play.

Next, scan the music of *Lavender's Blue*. The time signature is $\frac{3}{4}$ time, the music is played moderately fast, and you begin playing *mf* or *moderately loud*. At the beginning of the bottom line there is a *diminuendo* sign which means to *play gradually softer* leading to a *p* or *soft* in the next to last measure. See the *ritardando,* also in the next to last measure? It was introduced on page 91 and means to *gradually slow down,* in this case, to the end of the piece.

Also notice the 2 fermata signs over the dotted half notes in the last measure. Hold those notes for longer than their value of 3 beats. How long? Well, that's your decision. I would hold it for about 5 beats. There is also a pedal sign under the last 2 measures so this will create a nice, musical ending to *Lavender's Blue.*

The song starts with a melodic 5th in the RH and a C chord in the left. In the 3rd measure, the LH plays an F chord. Look at the bass staff, second line, 3rd measure. You will be playing descending harmonic intervals: a 6th, a 5th, a 4th, and then a 3rd in the following measure. When you play, remember to count and play evenly.

In *LAVENDER'S BLUE,* 5ths and 6ths are played with 1 & 5.
Practice this warm-up before playing *LAVENDER'S BLUE.*

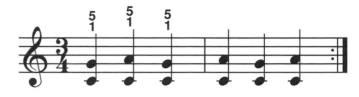

LAVENDER'S BLUE

C POSITION + 1

Moderately fast

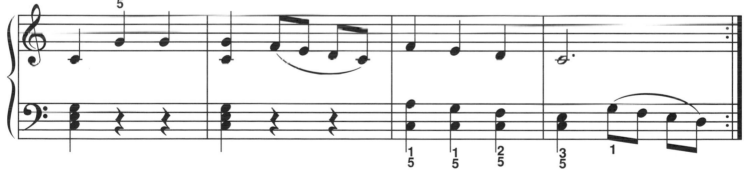

NEW TIME SIGNATURE

As you can see in the pink box at the right top of page 103, a $\frac{2}{4}$ time signature merely means there are 2 beats or counts in each measure and a quarter note receives 1 beat. As you already know $\frac{3}{4}$ and $\frac{4}{4}$ time, the only difference here is that there are only 2 beats in a measure rather than 3 or 4.

KUM-BA-YAH!

Kum-ba-yah is not only a very well-known spiritual, but a musically interesting one as well. The first thing that really stands out in the music is the changing time signatures. Look at the 1st line. It starts in $\frac{2}{4}$ time, which is new, and after one measure, changes to $\frac{4}{4}$ time, only to change right back again to $\frac{2}{4}$ time. This pattern of alternating time signatures continues for the whole song.

I really like this spiritual. Musically, it has so much to offer. The changing time signatures in every measure are truly unique. When a time signature changes in a piece, it usually changes just once and then changes back to the original time signature a little later. As you can now see, though a time signature is always placed at the beginning of a piece, it can also appear at the beginning of a measure anywhere within the piece.

Kum-ba-yah is played *moderately slow,* and if you look right under the *moderately slow* sign over the first measure, you'll see *2nd time both hands 8va,* meaning to play both hands an octave higher on the repeat. To make *Kum-ba-yah* really sound good, observe the slur marks and phrase accordingly.

Another important thing to watch is that you play both hands precisely together. You will be playing harmonic intervals in both hands and while it is always important to play hands precisely together, the music will not sound attractive if the harmonic intervals are not played together. Don't be too hard on yourself if you can't do this right away as it will take a little time.

When you feel comfortable playing the music, sing the lyrics as you play. *Kum-Ba-Yah* is really enjoyable to play and sing.

Self-Teaching Study Guide

KUM-BA-YAH!* 🔊

WITH CHANGING TIME SIGNATURES

Moderately slow

2nd time both hands 8va

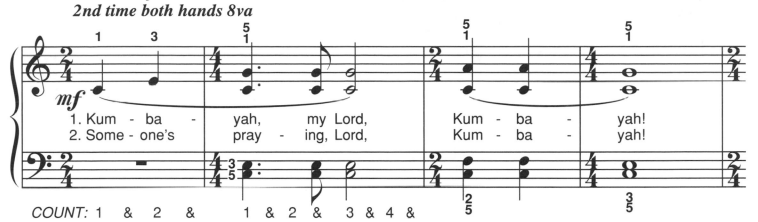

COUNT: 1 & 2 &   1 & 2 & 3 & 4 &

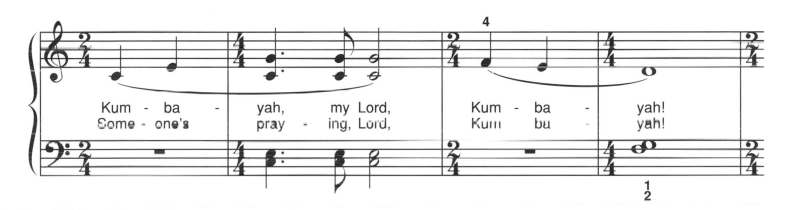

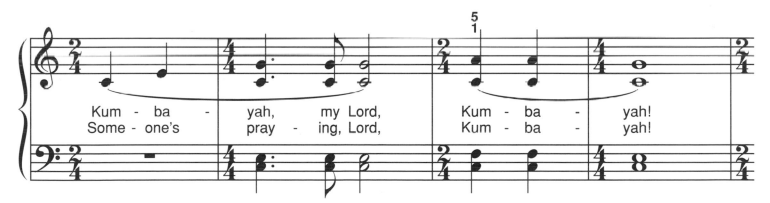

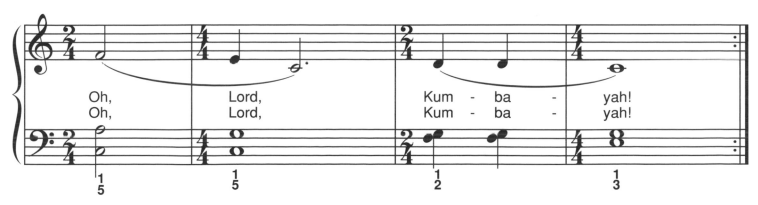

Kum-ba-yah means "Come by here."

Starting on page 99, you began moving away from playing in a set 5-finger position with each finger assigned to one key. With the introduction of 6ths, you expanded the range by one key to 6, with one finger in each hand assigned two keys. LH finger 1 played two keys and RH finger 5 played two keys. Now you are going to slightly expand this concept by having RH finger 1 also play two keys.

LONDON BRIDGE

On page 105, you will learn to play two very familiar folk songs, *London Bridge* and *Michael, Row the Boat Ashore*. In both of these songs, RH finger 1 will play C and D. The thumb can move very easily away from the 2nd finger, so this will not be a problem for you.

In *London Bridge*, the LH plays the C and G7 chords with LH finger 5 stretching down to B for the G7 chord. Before you start, place your hands on the keyboard as shown in the top keyboard diagram. Your LH will be in C Position so first move your 5th finger down to B and then back up to C. Next place RH finger 1 on D with fingers 2, 3, 4 and 5 on E, F, G and A. Then move your 1st finger down to C and back up to D. Play through *London Bridge* a few times while counting to yourself.

There are a few things to be aware of when you play. The LH starts with a C chord that is tied through the 2nd measure; it happens again in the second line. There is a repeat sign at the end of the song but on the repeat, the RH plays an octave higher than written. In the last measure, RH 2 plays E and then RH 1 skips a key to play C. The interval is a 3rd. This is the first time a finger has skipped a key. You will also skip the same key (D) in *Michael, Row the Boat Ashore* below. Remember to play the slurred notes smoothly connected. Other than that, you should be able to learn this piece quickly.

MICHAEL, ROW THE BOAT ASHORE

In *Michael, Row the Boat Ashore* on the lower half of the page, the RH is almost in the same position as it was for *London Bridge*, with the 1st finger playing C and the 2nd finger skipping D and playing E. Basically you are playing a melodic interval of a 3rd with fingers 1 and 2. The LH starts with a harmonic interval of a 4th with fingers 5 and 2, then continues with the melody. Once again, play the slurred notes smoothly connected. Notice you will start with an incomplete measure. Where are the missing 2 beats? I know I don't have to tell you that answer anymore.

When you play in positions that include six or more
notes, any finger may be required to play two notes.

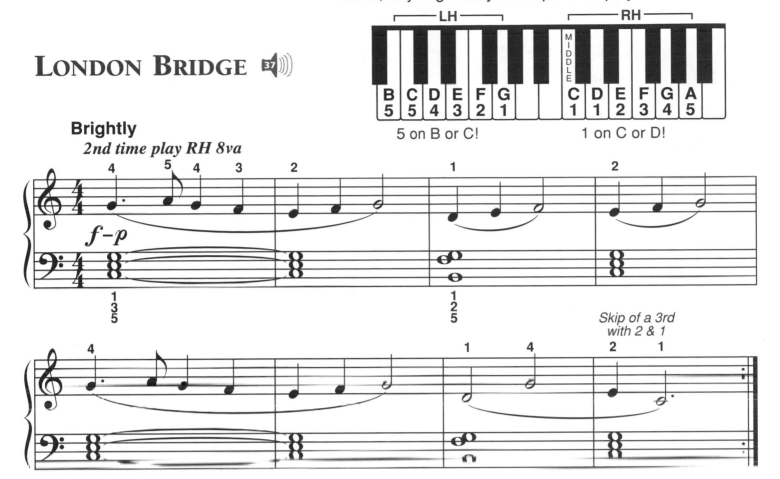

LONDON BRIDGE

Brightly
2nd time play RH 8va

MICHAEL, ROW THE BOAT ASHORE

RH 1 plays C, RH 2 plays E.

Moderately slow

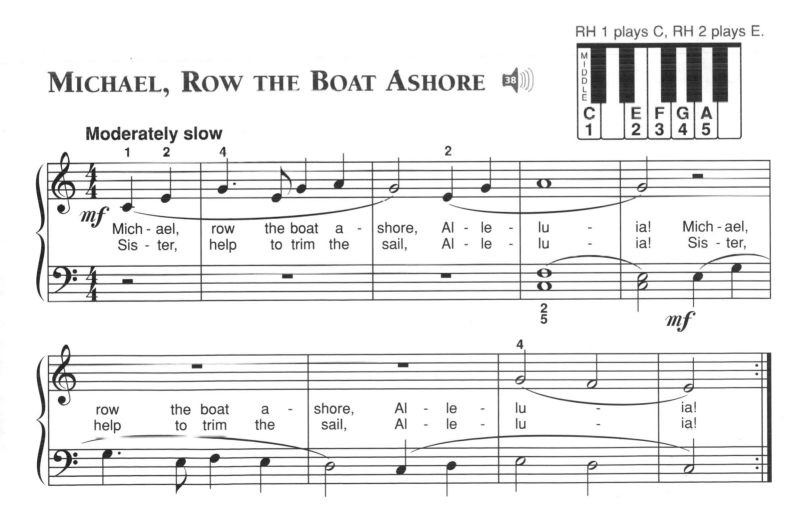

BLOW THE MAN DOWN!

Blow the Man Down! includes almost everything you've played before. RH finger 1 will play C and D. The LH will play broken chord versions of the C chord from measure 1 through measure 6, and then the G7 chord, starting in the last measure of the second line, and then continuing until the next to last measure. While you haven't played the broken C and G7 chords exactly this way, you have played broken chords in this style in *Beautiful Brown Eyes* on page 75.

Scan the music first and see what catches your eye. The song begins with an incomplete measure, nothing new here. In measures 2, 4, and 15, notice you'll be playing the RH melodic 3rds with fingers 1 and 2. In the bottom line, 1st measure, there are *fermata* signs over both staffs—hold the G7 chord in the LH and the A in the RH a little longer than their value. It makes for a nice dramatic pause. You'll also slow down in the last complete measure because of the *ritardando* sign.

When you perform this song, first count and play, then play and sing. When you feel you can play *Blow the Man Down* easily, begin your next practice session by playing the three songs you've just learned, one after the other— *London Bridge, Michael, Row the Boat Ashore* and *Blow the Man Down*! It will help develop flexibility, strength and stamina in your fingers and hands.

BLOW THE MAN DOWN!

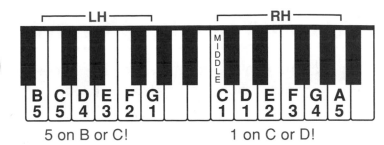

5 on B or C!   1 on C or D!

Moderately fast

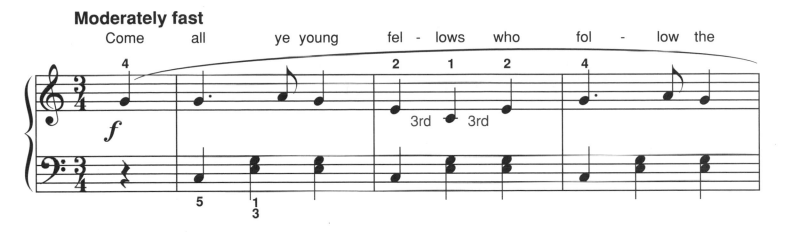

Come all ye young fel - lows who fol - low the

sea, Sing-ing "Way! Hey! Blow the man

down!" And please pay at - ten - tion and lis - ten to

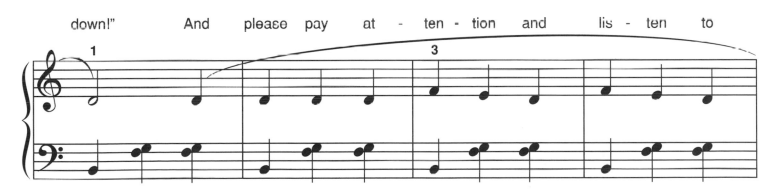

me; Give us some time to blow the man down!

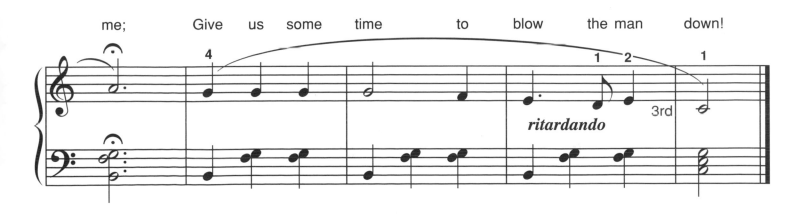

ritardando

108

Harmonic Interval Review

This is a writing page. It's not absolutely necessary but it is a very good review of the harmonic intervals you've learned so far.

1. Draw lines connecting the dots on the matching boxes.

2. Write the interval name (2, 3, 4, 5 or 6) on the line to the right of the music.

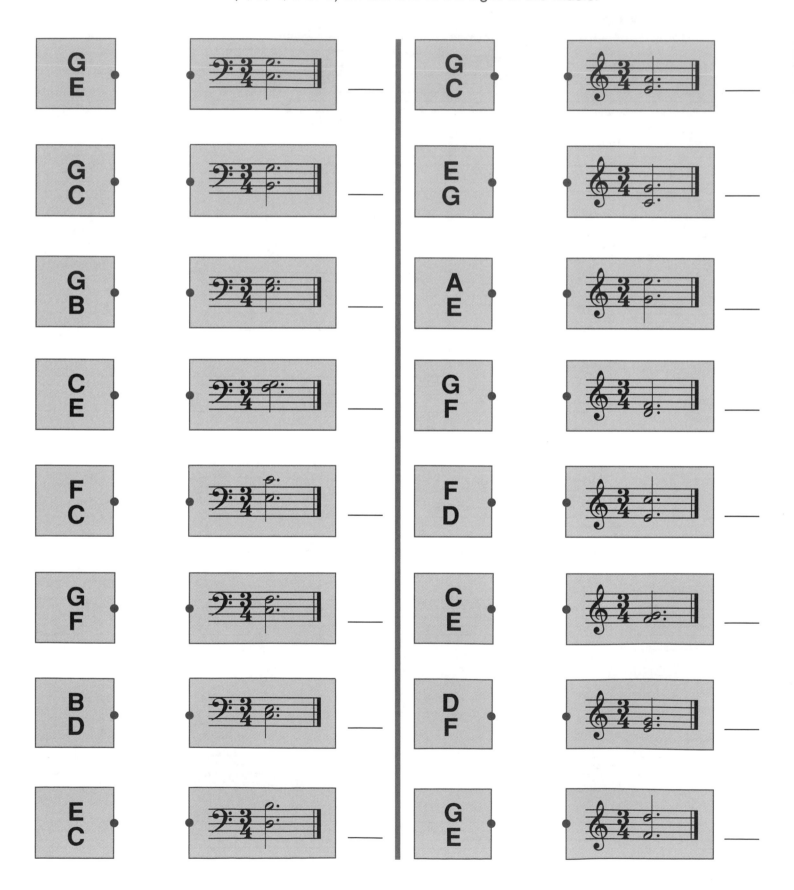

Moving Up & Down the Keyboard in 6ths

Moving Up & Down the Keyboard in 6ths on the lower half of this page is an exercise that will prepare you to move around the keyboard. Read the text under the title *Moving Up & Down the Keyboard in 6ths* below, then look at the first line of music.

To play these moving harmonic 6ths, keep your RH fingers in a set position while your hand moves up and down the keyboard. After you play the first harmonic 6th (C-A), keep your RH fingers in a 6th position, then play each successive 6th. You need only to read the bottom note because RH finger 5 will automatically go to the correct key.

Now look at the second line of music. Once again, to play these moving harmonic 6ths, keep your LH fingers in a set position while your hand moves up and down the keyboard. After you play the first harmonic 6th (E-C), keep your LH fingers in a 6th position, then play each successive 6th. You need only read the bottom note because LH finger 1 will automatically go to the correct key. Now play lines 1 and 2, counting aloud the first time, and then to yourself on the repeat.

Moving Up & Down the Keyboard in 6ths

To play popular and classical music, you must be able to move freely over the keyboard. These exercises will prepare you to do this. Each hand plays 6ths, moving up and down the keyboard to neighboring keys. READ ONLY THE LOWEST NOTE OF EACH INTERVAL, adding a 6th above!

RH 6ths, MOVING FROM $\begin{smallmatrix}A\\C\end{smallmatrix}$ **UP TO** $\begin{smallmatrix}E\\G\end{smallmatrix}$ **AND BACK.**

Begin with RH 1 on MIDDLE C.

LH 6ths, MOVING FROM $\begin{smallmatrix}C\\E\end{smallmatrix}$ **DOWN TO** $\begin{smallmatrix}F\\A\end{smallmatrix}$ **AND BACK.**

Begin with LH 1 on MIDDLE C.

LONE STAR WALTZ

Lone Star Waltz, on the lower half of this page, uses moving harmonic 6ths along with something new. Look at the pink box at the top of page 111 and you will see an explanation of a new term, *staccato. Staccato* means to play the note short and crisp. To indicate a *staccato*, a dot is placed over or under a note or notes.

Look at the bass staff in the top 2 music lines of page 111. The LH plays 2nds and 3rds in *staccato* style, meaning very short. The same thing occurs in the bottom 2 lines of music, but now in the treble staff with the RH.

Waltzes are always in ¾ time and *Lone Star Waltz* is no exception. If you look at the last measure on the bottom of page 111, you will see *D. C. al Fine.* This means you will return to the beginning of the piece and play it again, ending at *Fine (End),* which is at the bottom of this page. Right under "Moderate waltz tempo" above the first line of music, you will see that on the repeat, you will be playing both hands *8va,* one octave higher.

The first dynamic sign at the beginning of the piece is *piano* and you will play softly until the top of the next page. You will then play the RH 6ths *forte* and the LH 2nds and 3rds *mezzo forte.* When you get to the third line, the dynamic signs change again, with the LH playing *mezzo forte* and the RH playing *piano.* On the repeat at the beginning of the piece, you will return to *piano* again. Also on the repeat, you will slow down gradually in the next to the last measure of this page, indicated by the *ritardando* sign.

Now you are ready to begin. *Lone star Waltz* sounds a little like country music and should be a lot of fun to play.

LONE STAR WALTZ 🔊

This piece combines the positions used in *LONDON BRIDGE* with *Moving Up & Down the Keyboard in 6ths.*

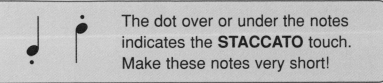

The dot over or under the notes indicates the **STACCATO** touch. Make these notes very short!

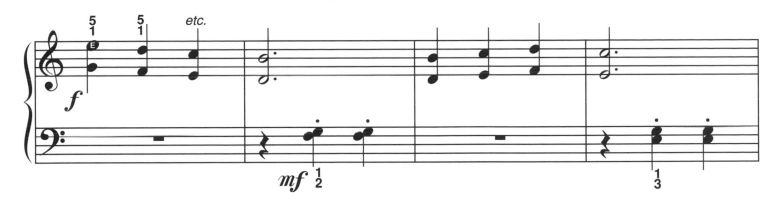

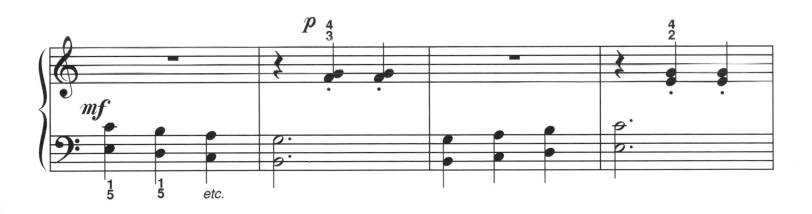

D. C. al Fine

Here is another lesson that will expand your ability to play a wider span of notes. First you played only 5ths, and recently we expanded that to 6ths. Now we are going to go about as far as you'll probably ever have to stretch.

Measuring 7ths & Octaves

The title of page 113 is *Measuring 7ths & Octaves*. While I know you know what 7th means, do you remember that on page page 86 you learned the meaning of the word *octave?* In music we use *octave*, a Latin word meaning 8, when we describe the interval of an 8th.

If you look at the left side of the page below the title, you will see a keyboard without any black keys displaying the span of a 7th. Counting the first key on the left as 1, count each key until you reach 7. The last key on the right is an interval of a 7th.

Now look at the right side of the page and you will see another keyboard, this time displaying the span of an *octave*. Once again, counting the first key on the left as 1, count each key until you get to 8. The last key on the right is an interval of an *octave*.

Look at the pink box on the left of the page and you will see what an interval of a 7th looks like on a staff. Whatever note you are playing on the staff, whether you go up or down, you will be going either from a line note to another line note, or a space note to another space note.

Now look at the pink box on the right of the page and you will see what an interval of an octave looks like on a staff. Whatever note you are playing on the staff, whether you go up or down, you will either be going from a line note to a space note, or a space note to a line note.

An interesting thing about octaves is that when you go up or down an octave, you are going from a lettered note to the same lettered note—C goes to a C, D to a D, etc. See the last measure of the first complete line of music on page 113. That's a C going to a higher C.

It's a bit of a stretch if you have a small hand and if you find it too difficult, lift finger RH 1 off the lower key and land on the higher key with your 5th finger. I do not want you to stretch your fingers if it is uncomfortable for you to do so. In time, your hand may gradually stretch but if not, don't worry about it. Just lift off the lower key and land on the higher key.

To work your way up to playing 7ths and octaves, you will slowly stretch as you play each higher interval on the lines of music below the pink boxes. The RH starts by playing melodic intervals from 2nds to octaves in the first line of music, followed by the playing of harmonic intervals in the second line of music. If you can't reach the harmonic octave, play it as a melodic interval.

Let's now get the LH involved with melodic and harmonic intervals in the third and fourth lines of music, in the same way you played the RH melodic and harmonic intervals. When you complete the bottom line, review this page by playing through the whole page again.

Measuring 7ths & Octaves

When you skip 5 white keys,
the interval is a **7th**.

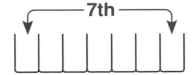

When you skip 6 white keys,
the interval is an **OCTAVE.**

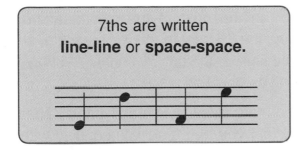

7ths are written
line-line or **space-space.**

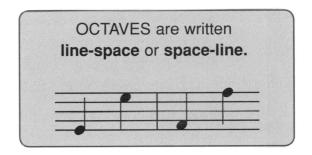

OCTAVES are written
line-space or **space-line.**

Say the names of these intervals as you play!

RH MELODIC INTERVALS

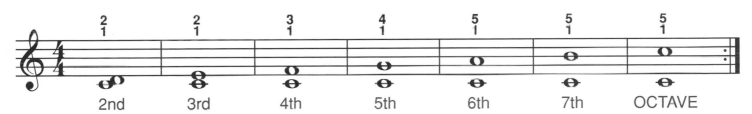

RH HARMONIC INTERVALS

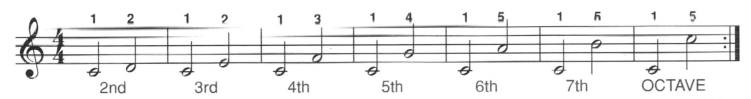

LH MELODIC INTERVALS

LH HARMONIC INTERVALS

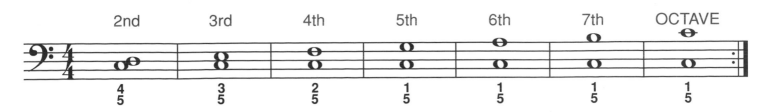

CAFÉ VIENNA

Café Vienna, on page 115, uses all the intervals from 2nds to the octave except a 4th. The RH includes 3rds, 5ths, 6ths, 7ths, and an octave in the final measure (C to C). The LH includes harmonic 2nds and 3rds. If you are in the mood, make yourself some espresso and imagine you are in Vienna on the *Ringstrasse* looking at the *Vienna Opera House.*

Scan the music first. Notice that the first 6 measures of the top 2 lines and the first 6 measures of the bottom 2 lines are exactly the same. There is an important difference, however, in the last 2 measures of line 2 and line 4.

A shift in your RH position takes place in the next to the last measure of the piece. Beginning at line 4, just after playing the 3rd beat in the 2nd measure, shift your RH to the left to play G in the following measure with your 5th finger. You may want to first concentrate on the bottom line when you play this piece.

Though I haven't mentioned it recently, start by playing each hand separately—that's always recommended unless you feel you can start immediately with hands together. The better you get at sight reading, the more easily you will be able to start this way. Professional pianists can frequently play from music as easily as you read from a book.

When you play this page, let your imagination place you in a happy scene. *Café Vienna* is an attractive piece that will make you feel like you are eating some strudel in Vienna. To be a good musician, you must also have a good imagination—and you won't add any calories this way.

CAFÉ VIENNA

Play hands separately at first, then together.

Be especially careful of the RH fingering!

Notice that the first two notes, a melodic 3rd, are played with 2 & 1!

Moderate waltz tempo

The Flat Sign

Previously, on page 63, you have learned that when you see a sharp sign before a note, it means to play the next *higher* key to the right, whether black or white. It probably comes as no surprise that there is another symbol that means to play the next *lower* key to the left, whether black or white. That symbol is a *flat* sign and you can see it at the top left side of page 117. Its definition is right beside it. Note the keyboard chart in the middle of the page that shows a white key B and a lower, black key, B♭. That is an example of how a flat sign would affect the note B and lower it to a B♭.

Look at the top right of this page and read the red text. It explains that just like a sharp, when a flat sign appears before a note, it applies to that same note if it appears again in the measure. The treble staff below the text consists of 3 measures. In the 1st measure, there is a B♭. Because a bar line cancels a flat sign, the first note of the 2nd measure needs to have a flat sign if it is to be played as a B♭. The second B in that measure is also played as a flat but does not need to have a flat sign because the flat sign still applies. The last measure is obviously played as a B♭.

ROCK IT AWAY!

Rock It Away! is a fun rock song that contains some B flats. See the B♭ in the 4th measure of line 1 of the treble staff? The bar line at the end of the measure cancels the flat sign. Look at the 1st measure of the next line and you'll see another B. This B is played as a white key because the flat in the previous measure was cancelled by the following bar line.

As you scan the music, notice that the LH consists only of chords: G, C and D7, and played as whole notes. Some of the whole note chords are tied and held for 2 measures. The exception is in the next to the last measure where the C and D7 chords are played as half notes. In this piece, you play flats in the RH and sharps in the LH. There is one measure that contains both a flat and a sharp—can you find it?

Start by playing the RH first, then play the bass chords, and finally put both hands together. The tempo is moderately fast and played *moderately loud* throughout. Try to smoothly connect all the notes under the slur marks.

The Flat Sign

The **FLAT SIGN** before a note means play the next key to the LEFT, whether black or white!

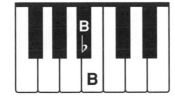

When a FLAT (♭) appears before a note, it applies to that note for the rest of the measure.

Circle the notes that are FLAT:

ROCK IT AWAY!

Moderately fast

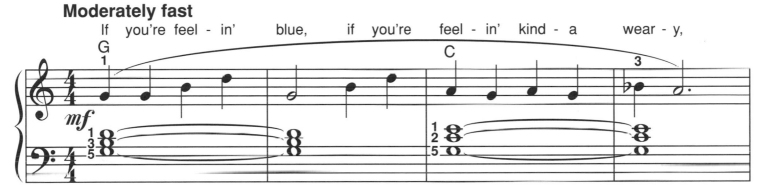

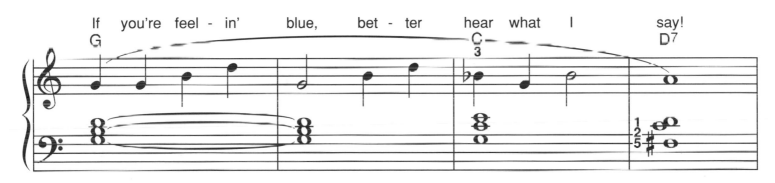

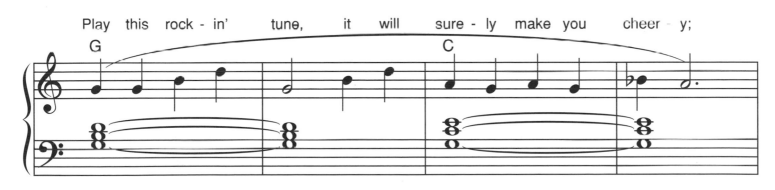

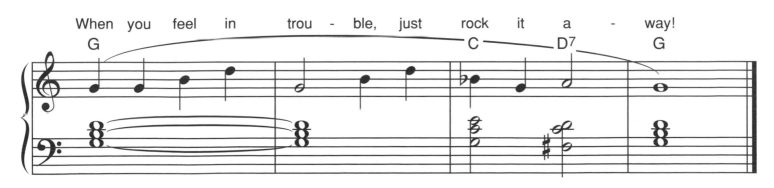

Measuring Half Steps & Whole Steps

Half Steps & Whole Steps form the core of all theory, and are the basic stepping stones of music itself.

Half Steps

Under the red *Half Steps* on page 119 is a definition of the term. A *half step* is the distance from any key to the very next key above or below, whether black or white. Look at the top keyboard chart to the right. Notice the small red text above the chart as it highlights the half steps. From C, the next higher key is a black key or C sharp, a half step *higher*. The next half step higher is white key D. If you lower the D with a flat sign, you get a D♭, a half step *lower*. As you can see, C♯ and D♭ are the same key.

Point with your index finger to each key at the top of the page and say the note name for each half step from C to F: C to C♯, C♯ to D, D to D♯, D♯ to E, and, not surprisingly, E to F, a half step. Now that's interesting. There are actually two places on the keyboard where white keys are not separated by a black key—E and F, and B and C.

Whole Steps

Under the red *Whole Steps* on page 119 is a definition of the term. A whole step consists of 2 half steps. It skips a key above or below a note, whether black or white. Look at the middle keyboard chart to the right. Notice the small red text above the chart as it highlights the whole steps. From C, and skipping C♯, is D, a whole step higher. You are always going to skip a key as you move up or down by whole steps.

Once again, point with your index finger to each labeled key in the middle of the page and say the note name for the whole steps from C to A♯/B♭: C to D (skipping a black key), D to E (skipping a black key), E to F♯ (skipping a white key), F♯ to G♯ (skipping a white key), and G♯ to A♯ (skipping a white key). When you understand all this you will be well on your way to completely understanding the basics of music theory.

Tetrachords

Now you are going to put half steps and whole steps together to construct a basic music pattern, the *Tetrachord*. Look near the bottom of the page at the Tetrachords section. *Tetra* is the Latin word for 4 so a *tetrachord* is a series of 4 notes having a specific pattern of whole step, whole step, half step.

Look at the keyboard chart at the bottom of the page. In building a *tetrachord*, it is important that the notes be in alphabetical order. Notice the small red text at the top of the keyboard as it highlights the steps: whole step, whole step, half step. Point to the keys of the chart, again with your index finger, and say the keys and the steps: C to D (a whole step), D to E (a whole step), E to F (a half step).

And there you have it, the *tetrachord*, an important building block and the foundation of the very important *major scale*.

Measuring Half Steps & Whole Steps

Half Steps

A **HALF STEP** is the distance from any key to the very next key above or below (black or white).

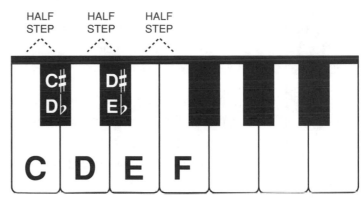

HALF STEPS • NO KEY BETWEEN

Whole Steps

A **WHOLE STEP** is equal to 2 half steps. Skip one key (black or white).

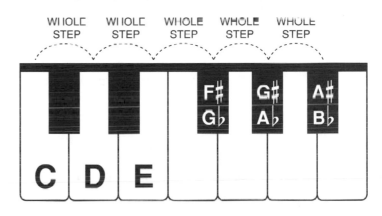

WHOLE STEPS • ONE KEY BETWEEN

Tetrachords

A **TETRACHORD** is a series of FOUR NOTES having a pattern of

WHOLE STEP, WHOLE STEP, HALF STEP.

The notes of a tetrachord must be in alphabetical order →

and must also have this pattern! →

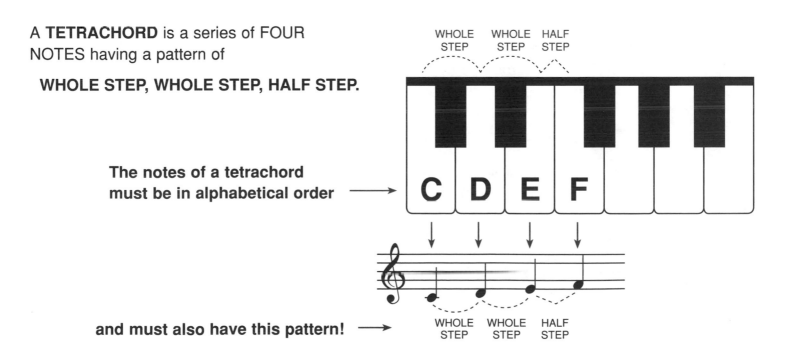

The Major Scale

The Major Scale on page 121 is a big step forward in learning to play the piano. To form a major scale with the RH, take one 4-note tetrachord, skip a whole step, and then add another 4-note tetrachord above it. The two tetrachords add up to 8 notes, and that is the major scale. Can it be this easy? Well, yes and no. The mental understanding of how a scale is formed will be easy for you—but performing the scale involves some new fingerings.

First, the easy part. Read the first two lines of text under the title, and then look at the music. The first tetrachord begins on C, and is a C tetrachord. The second tetrachord begins on G, and is a G tetrachord. The last note of the first tetrachord (F) and the first note of the second tetrachord (G) are separated by a whole step. Knowing this rule, you can form a major scale beginning on any note on the keyboard, whether black or white. Now that's a lot of learning in a very short time. You can try this after we complete the page, but for now let's work our way through to actually playing a major scale.

Preparation for Scale Playing

There is a clever exercise under *Preparation for Scale Playing*. It will prepare you for the movement of the 1st and 3rd fingers in scale playing. As there are 8 notes in a scale and we only have 5 fingers, there must be a trick to it. There is. You must first *pass* your 1st finger *under* your 3rd finger as you ascend the tetrachord with the RH—and then *cross* your 3rd finger *over* the 1st finger as you descend the tetrachord.

Play measures 1 and 2 of the first complete line of music. The red text between measures 1 and 2 tells you to pass your 1st finger or thumb *under* your 3rd finger as you move *up* or ascend the tetrachord to play F. Then play measures 3 and 4. The red text over the 3rd measure tells you to cross your 3rd finger *over* your 1st finger to play E as you move *down* or descend the tetrachord. This is an important preparation for scale playing so play this exercise quite a few times before moving to the LH.

On the next line of music, you'll do the same thing except you'll be playing with your LH. Read the red text under the staff for directions on passing 1 under 3 as you *descend* the tetrachord and cross 3 over 1 as you *ascend* the tetrachord. Play this exercise quite a few times also until you have mastered the finger movements.

The C Major Scale

Read the text under *The C Major Scale* title. Begin slowly and lean the hand slightly in the direction you are moving. Very importantly, the hands should move smoothly along with no twisting of the wrist. You already know the hard part of the bottom 2 lines of music, the first and last measures of each exercise. The middle measures are simply playing out fingers 2–5 in both hands. Repeat each exercise until you can play the scale notes smoothly and evenly.

Playing scales properly is the foundation for becoming a fine pianist, and I hope you take this exercise seriously and practice it every day.

The Major Scale

The MAJOR SCALE is made of **TWO TETRACHORDS** *joined* by a **WHOLE STEP.**

The C MAJOR SCALE is constructed as follows:

KEY-NOTE   WHOLE STEP   KEY-NOTE

WHOLE WHOLE HALF   WHOLE WHOLE HALF

└— **1st TETRACHORD** —┘   └—**2nd TETRACHORD**—┘

> There is no ♯ or ♭ in the **C MAJOR SCALE.**

Each scale begins and ends on a note of the same name as the scale, called the **KEY NOTE.**

Preparation for Scale Playing

IMPORTANT! Since there are **8** notes in the C major scale and we only have **5** fingers, an important trick must be mastered: **passing the thumb under the 3rd finger!** This exercise will make this trick easy.

Play HANDS SEPARATELY. Begin VERY SLOWLY. Keep the wrist loose and quiet!

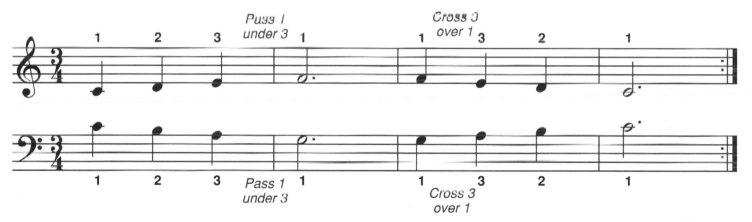

The C Major Scale

Begin SLOWLY. *Lean* the hand slightly in the direction you are moving.
The hand should move smoothly along, with no twisting motion of the wrist!

JOY TO THE WORLD

A major scale can be a thing of beauty. *Joy to the World* on page 123 is a very popular Christmas song and it is largely based on a major scale. It was composed by George Frideric Handel, one of the most important composers of the Baroque period. He wrote many fine works including the *Messiah*, which includes the incredible *Hallelujah Chorus*.

If you have been practicing your scales, playing *Joy to the World* will be easy for you. What's new is a dynamic sign shown in the pink box in the upper right corner of the page. It is *fortissimo*, a beautiful Italian word, that means to play *very loud*. There is a difference, however, between banging loudly and playing loudly. When you play *fortissimo*, hold back a little. Let your ear judge whether you are playing musically or just very, very loud. You can also hurt your finger by playing too loud. As time goes by, you will gain strength in your fingers but until then, play under control.

The key to success in performing *Joy to the World* is to pay very special attention to the dynamic signs. The scale portions should present very little problems for you. The bottom line has a RH octave interval and the LH has some C and G7 chords in the bottom 2 bass lines. As always, play the notes under the slurs smoothly. There are also a few pedal marks to watch and one *crescendo* sign leading up to *fortissimo* in the 2nd measure of the second line.

Other than that, go to it. I would recommend to first start practicing by playing hands separately, then hands together.

JOY TO THE WORLD 🔊

Scales occur often in melodies. This favorite melody is made up almost entirely of major scales.

NEW DYNAMIC SIGN

$\boldsymbol{f\!f}$ *(fortissimo)* = very loud

George Frideric Handel

More About Chords

While page 125, *More About Chords,* does have some playing involved, it is mostly going to be an explanatory page. Now that you have learned the C major scale, we can start to explain how chords are formed. This page begins with an explanation of a *triad*—merely a basic 3-note chord. Notice the 3 pink boxes that include the words root, third and fifth at the top of the page. To the right of the boxes are the notes of a triad. The bottom note is the *root* of the triad, the middle note is an interval of a 3rd up from the root, and the top note is an interval of a 5th up from the root. They are also the 1st, 3rd and 5th notes of the major scale. The root gives the triad its name. As the root of this triad is C, it is, therefore, called a C triad or C chord.

Look at the next lower row of triads. When a triad is in a root position, they will either look like the triad on the left, with the notes *on* the lines, or like the triad on the right, with the notes *in* the spaces. Notice the notes are named going up from the bottom note to the top note—root, 3rd, 5th. A chord is usually read from the bottom up. Finally, a triad can be built on any note of any scale.

TRIADS BUILT ON THE C MAJOR SCALE

Under the heading *Triads Built on the C Major Scale* is a music line of triads for the RH. The first triad is a C triad, so named after its root; the second is a D triad, and so on. The fingering is usually 1-3-5. The roots of all the triads on this line make up the C major scale. Put your RH in a 1-3-5 position and play each triad going up the C major scale.

The second line of music shows the triads of the LH. I would like you to play this line for the LH, exactly as you played the first line for the RH.

When you name the notes of a triad in root position, you will always skip one letter of the musical alphabet between each note. In the C major scale, the C triad is C-E-G; the D triad D-F-A; the E triad E-G-B, etc. Play the two lines of music several times. For fun, try playing the two lines of triads with hands together.

More About Chords

A TRIAD IS A 3-NOTE CHORD.

The three notes of a triad are:

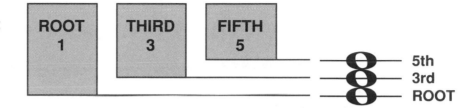

The ROOT is the note from which the triad gets its name. The root of a C triad is C.

Triads in **ROOT POSITION** (with root at the bottom) always look like this:

Triads may be built on any note of any scale.

TRIADS BUILT ON THE C MAJOR SCALE

Play with RH:

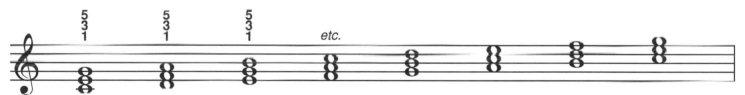

Play with LH:

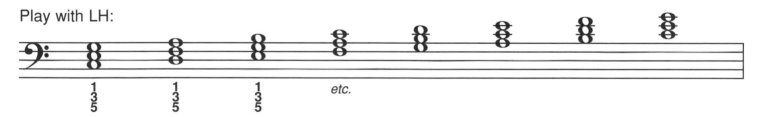

Listen carefully to the sound of these root position triads!

When you name the notes of any **TRIAD IN ROOT POSITION,** you will always skip **ONE** letter of the musical alphabet between each note. The triads you played above are:

C E G   D F A   E G B   F A C   G B D   A C E   B D F

This is the complete **"TRIAD VOCABULARY."** It should be memorized!

There is some new theory introduced on page 127. Read the text under the title *Cockles and Mussels*. When music is based on a scale, it is said to be in the key of that scale. As the C major scale does not use any sharps or flats and as the melody begins and ends on the note C, *Cockles and Mussels* is said to be in the key of C major.

COCKLES AND MUSSELS

Cockles and Mussels is an attractive Irish folk song about sweet Molly Malone. Notice how the triads are used in the bass clef, very much like the exercise you just played at the bottom of page 125. The tied triads are held for either 5 or 6 beats. *Cockles and Mussels* is in $\frac{3}{4}$ time and the 1st measure is incomplete—check the last measure for the missing beats. The tempo is moderately slow and the dynamic sign indicates *mezzo forte*, moderately loud.

A quick scan through the music indicates nothing special to watch out for until you reach the last 2 measures. In the next-to-last measure, there is a *ritardando* (gradually slow down) and a *diminuendo* (gradually play softer). In the last measure, there is a *fermata* (hold the notes longer) and a pedal marking.

I would suggest playing *Cockles and Mussels* hands separately at first, and then with both hands together. As the melody is in the RH, play the melody a little louder than the accompaniment. When you play, listen how beautiful the melody and accompaniment sound when they are played precisely together. Remember to sing the lyrics when you can play the music smoothly.

COCKLES AND MUSSELS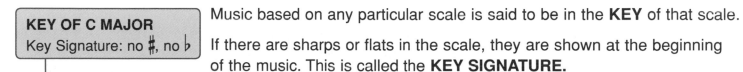

KEY OF C MAJOR
Key Signature: no #, no ♭

Music based on any particular scale is said to be in the **KEY** of that scale.

If there are sharps or flats in the scale, they are shown at the beginning of the music. This is called the **KEY SIGNATURE.**

Moderately slow

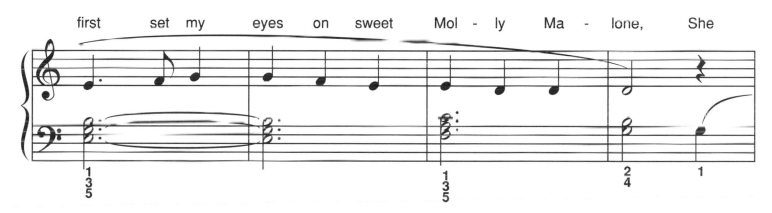

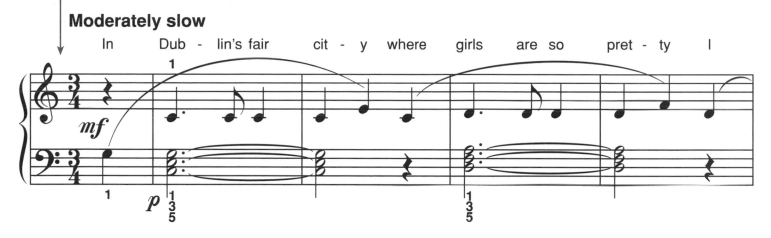

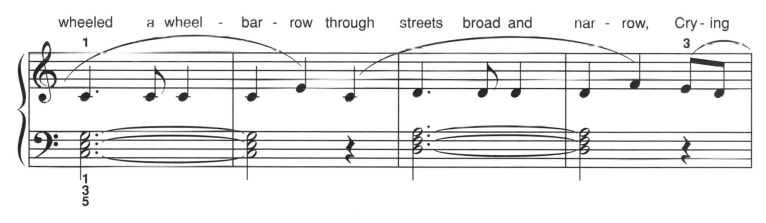

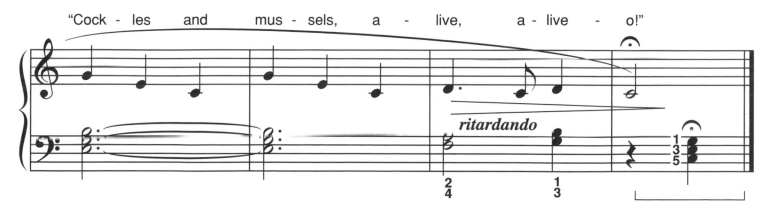

The Primary Chords in C Major

Please turn to page 129 to learn about *The Primary Chords in C Major*. This page is devoted to explaining how chords are formed and then how they are slightly altered to sound better and become easier to play. Read through the text at the top of the page until you reach the first line of music. The bottom notes on the staff form a C major scale. You can build a 3-note chord on every note of the scale. What the text basically says is that the 3 most important chords in any key are those built on the 1st, 4th and 5th notes of the scale. Because of that, they are called the *primary chords* and the bottom note of each chord is called the *root* of that chord.

When you change from one chord to another, it is called a *chord progression*. When all chords are in root position, the hand has to jump from one chord to the next. Play the I, IV and V7 (1, 4, 5-7) chords—they are the C, F, and G7 chords as written on the first line of music at the top of the page. See how separated the chords are on the keyboard?

Chord Progressions

Look at the next lower line of music, under the title *Chord Progressions*. The first chord is the I chord in root position—in this case—a C chord. You will not make any changes to this chord. Then look at the next chord to the right, the IV or F chord. See how the top note C is moved down an octave? It is still a IV chord but now the bottom note is no longer an F but a C.

The next chord to the right is a V7 chord. Because we want to keep all the primary chords limited to three notes each, we usually omit the 5th in the V7 chord, in this case a D. Compare this 3-note chord to the V7 chord in the top line of music. The chord now has only 3 notes rather than 4. Looking again at the V7 chord in the lower staff, also notice how the top 2 notes of this 3-note chord are lowered an octave. It is still a V7 chord but now the bottom note is no longer G but B.

The next lower line, the half line of music under the text, shows the 3 primary chords in their new positions. By making these note changes, playing the I, IV and V7 chords is easier and they sound more musical.

The I or C chord in root position is fingered 5-3-1. To move to the IV or F chord, the 5th finger stays on C, raise the 3rd finger off E, the 2nd finger will be on F, and the 1st finger will move up to A.

To move from the IV chord to the V7 or G7 chord, the 5th finger moves down to B, the 2nd finger remains on F, and the 1st finger moves down to G. Now play all 3 chords, one after the other. Finally, play the bottom line of music saying the chord names as you play. Play the bottom line quite a few times. Repeat until you are not only familiar with the notes, the fingerings, the names of the chords, but the *sound* of the chords.

The Primary Chords in C Major

The three most important chords in any key are those built on the 1st, 4th & 5th notes of the scale. These are called the **PRIMARY CHORDS** of the key.

The chords are identified by the Roman numerals **I**, **IV** & **V** (1, 4 & 5).
The **V** chord usually adds the note a 7th above the root to make a **V⁷** (say "5-7") chord.

In the key of C major, the **I** **CHORD** is the C MAJOR TRIAD.
The **IV** **CHORD** is the F MAJOR TRIAD.
The **V⁷** **CHORD** is the G⁷ CHORD (G major triad with an added 7th).

The Primary Chords in C Major

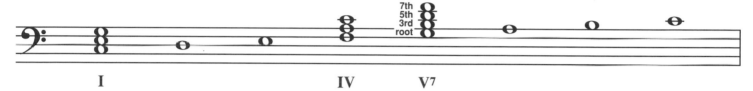

Chord Progressions

When we change from one chord to another, we call this a **CHORD PROGRESSION.**

When all chords are in root position, the hand must leap from one chord to the next. To make the chord progressions easier to play and sound better, the **IV** and **V⁷** chords may be played in other positions by moving one or more of the higher chord tones down an octave.

The **I** chord is played in ROOT POSITION:

The top note of the **IV** chord is moved down an octave:

In the **V⁷** chord, the 5th (D) is usually omitted. All notes except the root are moved down an octave:

The three PRIMARY CHORDS are then comfortably played as follows:

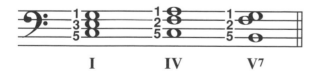

It is important that you now think of the C, F & G⁷ chords in the key of C MAJOR as the **I**, **IV** & **V⁷** chords!

Play the following line several times, saying the numerals of each chord as you play.

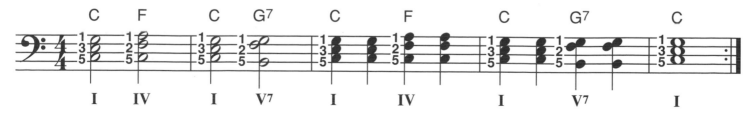

About the Blues

To learn about the blues form and how it is unique, read the top paragraph on page 131 under the title *About the Blues,* and then read the formula for the blues in the pink box. The musical form of the blues is a little different than the music you have been playing. There are usually 16 measures to a standard song but the blues has only 12. This is one example of the differences—there are more.

GOT THOSE BLUES

Playing *Got Those Blues* will be a real departure for you. Play the first line of music as written. How did that sound? Probably nice but a little stiff. To play the blues properly you have to loosen up a little—and how do you do that? The key is to play the pairs of 8th notes a bit unevenly, or a longer note followed by a shorter note, otherwise known as *long-short*. This is called "swinging the eighths" and sure enough, swing music is also played this way. If you say lah—de—dah—de—dah, you'll probably get the rhythm correct. At the bottom of the page is another explanation of the *long-short* rhythm.

When you play *Got Those Blues*, be sure to play the pairs of 8th notes *long-short* and you'll get a nice blues feel to the piece. I would suggest you begin your practice by playing the LH alone. You should be able to play the chord progressions smoothly as you already played them at the bottom of page 129.

Play the staccato notes in both hands crisply and be sure to keep a steady beat. Watch the dynamics signs as they get softer and then louder. The last measure has a nice ending—slow down and hold the last chord a little longer. It's a great piece and I know you will enjoy performing it.

About the Blues

Music called **BLUES** has long been a part of the American musical heritage. We find it in the music of many popular song writers, in ballads, boogie, and rock.

BLUES music follows a basic formula, that is, a standard chord progression. If you learn the formula for *GOT THOSE BLUES!* you will be able to play the blues in any key you learn, simply by applying the formula to that key.

Formula for the Blues

There are 12 measures in one chorus of the blues:

4 measures of the **I** chord
2 measures of the **IV** chord
2 measures of the **I** chord
1 measure of the **V⁷** chord
1 measure of the **IV** chord
2 measures of the **I** chord

GOT THOSE BLUES!

*The eighth notes may be played a bit unevenly:

long short long short, *etc.*

The Primary Chords in C Major

The 3 most important chords in any key are those built on the 1st, 4th and 5th notes of the scale. These are called the PRIMARY CHORDS of the key.

In many pieces a **V⁷** CHORD is used instead of a **V** TRIAD.
To make a **V⁷** chord, a note an interval of a 7th above the root is added to the **V** triad.

1. Circle the 1st, 4th and 5th notes of each of the scales below.
   These notes are the roots of the primary triads.

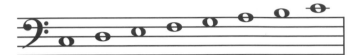
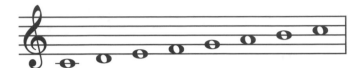

2. Write the names of the notes in each chord in the squares above the staff.
3. Circle the root of each chord on the staff.
4. Write the name of the chord (**I**, **IV** or **V⁷**) on the line below the staff.

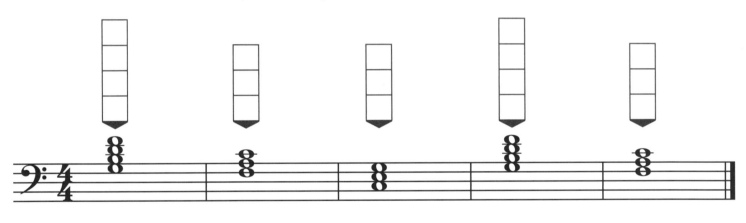

To make the chord progressions easier to play and sound better, the **IV** and **V⁷** chords may be played in other positions by moving one or more of the higher chord tones down an octave.

5. Write the names of the notes in each chord in the squares above the staff.
6. Circle the root of each chord on the staff.
7. Write the name of the chord (**I**, **IV** or **V⁷**) on the line below the staff.

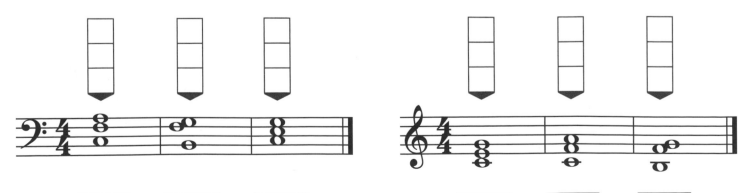

As your lessons have progressed, you gradually expanded the range of notes you were playing. You started with a span of 5 notes with the C Position, then added 6ths, 7ths, and finally the octave. On this page, you are going to learn to play in an extended position within the octave range.

RH: An Extended Position

Look at the keyboard chart on the bottom half of this page. As you now know, the first three keys, C-E-G, form a C chord. You are now going to add an additional C an octave higher than the root, C. The staff below the chart shows how the music is written to create an *Extended Position*.

Place your fingers on the piano and play C with the 1st finger. Then move up to E with your 2nd finger, lifting your 1st finger as you play E. Next comes the 3rd finger on G, lifting your 2nd finger as you play G. Last comes the 5th finger on the higher C, lifting your 3rd finger as you play C. To make this stretch easily, move your arm and wrist ever so slightly to the right as you play the G and C. Play these two measures several times until you can play the notes smoothly connected.

Look further down the page to *LH Review: Block Chords & Broken Chords in C*. You have already been playing block and broken chords. The LH of the piece you will be playing on the next page consists entirely of broken I, IV and V7 chords, in this case C, F and G7 chords. Play these block and broken chords several times until you feel comfortable playing the broken chords in a steady tempo. Playing the broken chords smoothly connected will help to make playing *On Top of Old Smoky* on page 134 so much more musical.

RH: An Extended Position

ON TOP OF OLD SMOKY begins and ends with the RH in an EXTENDED POSITION.

Play several times:

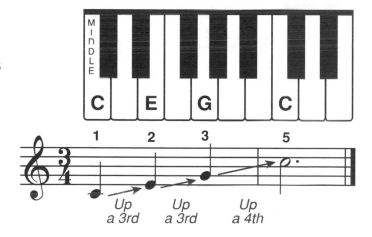

LH Review: Block Chords & Broken Chords in C

ON TOP OF OLD SMOKY

On Top of Old Smoky is a folk song that will probably sound familiar to you. *Smoky*, as you can guess by reading the lyrics, is a mountain. Notice the *pedal marks* beginning in the 2nd measure below and then appearing periodically throughout the song. The first *extended position* for the RH begins in the 1st measure of the song. It can also be found again in the last 2 measures of the bottom line on page 135. When you begin to play *Smoky*, however, I'd recommend you begin playing the LH first.

The song is in ¾ time and played at a moderately slow tempo. The dynamic sign *mf* indicates to play *moderately loud* and stays that way until the last two measures of the piece, where you play gradually softer because of the *diminuendo* sign. *On Top of Old Smoky* begins with an incomplete measure on this page and the missing two counts (half note) are found in the very last measure of page 135. The half notes have *fermatas* above them so hold those notes a little longer than usual. When you can put it all together, I'd like you to sing the song also.

ON TOP OF OLD SMOKY 🔊

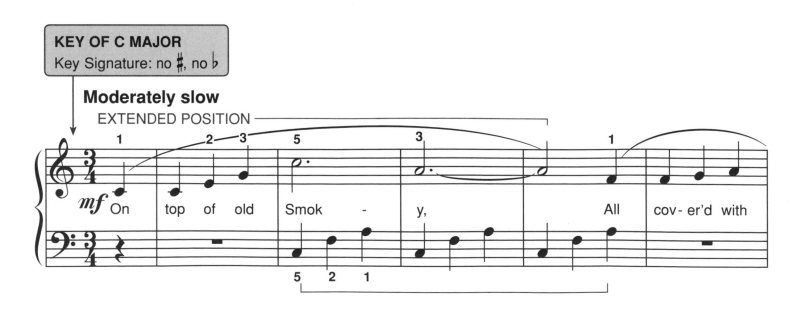

On page 121, you studied the C Major Scale. You learned that a major scale is made up of two *tetrachords* joined by a whole step. A *tetrachord*, you may remember, is made up of a whole step, another whole step, and a half step. You may want to take another look at that page before we proceed, but it is not absolutely necessary. Using this formula, you can create a major scale on any note, black or white, on the keyboard.

The G Major Scale

On page 137, you will now learn how to play the *G Major Scale*. Look at the top line of music on the page and you will see the G major scale. It obviously begins and ends on G. The first *tetrachord*, therefore, starts on G. It is then a whole step up to A, another whole step up to B, then a half step up to C. You are now going to move up a whole step to D to begin the second *tetrachord*. This *tetrachord* is very interesting. A whole step up from D is E, a whole step up from E is not F but F♯. A half step up from F♯ is G. What that means is that when playing in the key of G, all F's will be played sharp unless otherwise indicated. The high F♯ and G notes are new so pay special attention to them.

The Key of G Major

Read the text under the heading, *The Key of G Major*. The second paragraph explains that rather than writing a sharp sign before every F in a piece, a sharp sign can be placed after the clef sign. See the pink box titled Key of G Major? It shows you where the sharp sign is placed on the staff—this is known as the *key signature*. One of the first things you will always look at when playing a new piece is the *key signature*.

Next, look at the complete line of music under the pink box. This is the *ascending* G scale for the RH. Start on G with the 1st finger, then play A and B with fingers 2 and 3. Now pass the 1st finger under your 3rd finger to play C. You used this same fingering to play the C major scale. With your 1st finger on C, play the rest of the scale (D-E-F♯-G) with fingers 2-3-4-5. F♯ and G are new notes and they will be played by your 4th and 5th fingers. The key signature includes a sharp sign on the top line of the staff, the F line—therefore all F's in the music, wherever they are located, will be played sharp. Play the RH G scale several times, saying the note names as you play evenly.

The bottom line of music starts with the *descending* G scale for the LH. Play this scale the same way you played the *ascending* scale for the RH, once again saying the note names as you play. This time, however, you will pass finger 1 under 3 while descending, and cross finger 3 over 1 while ascending.

When you can play the G major scale with each hand, I would like you to play the scale with hands together in contrary motion. Read the text under the music and remember that the same numbered fingers on both hands play at the same time.

The G Major Scale

Remember that the MAJOR SCALE is made up of two tetrachords *joined* by a whole step.

The second TETRACHORD of the G MAJOR SCALE begins on D.

There is 1 sharp (F♯) in the **G MAJOR SCALE.**

The Key of G Major

A piece based on the G major scale is in the **KEY OF G MAJOR.**
Since F is sharp in the G scale, every F will be sharp in the key of G major.

Instead of placing a sharp before every F in the entire piece,
the sharp is indicated at the beginning in the KEY SIGNATURE.

KEY OF G MAJOR
Key Signature: 1 sharp (F♯)
Play all "F's" sharp throughout.

Practice the G major scale with HANDS SEPARATE.
Begin SLOWLY. Keep the wrist loose and quiet.

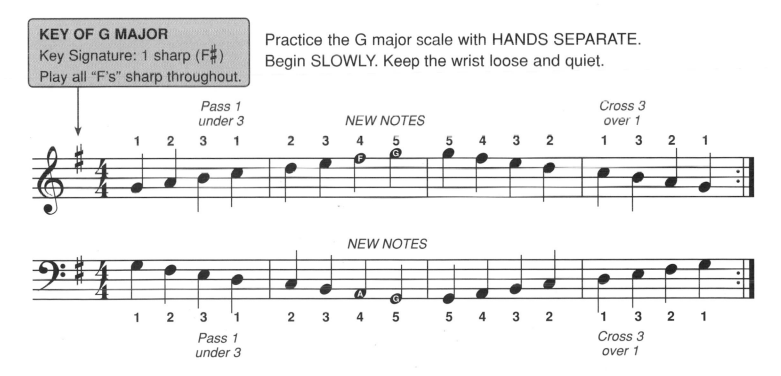

IMPORTANT! After you have learned the G MAJOR SCALE with hands separate, you may play the hands together. When the scale is played as written on the staffs above, the LH descends as the RH ascends, and vice versa. This is called CONTRARY MOTION—both hands play the *same numbered* fingers at the same time!

You may also play the C MAJOR SCALE at the bottom of page 121 with the hands together, in CONTRARY MOTION!

A New Trick!

On page 139, you will learn something new that is not difficult at all. You will learn to play a note with one finger, and then play the same note again with a different finger.

Look at the top line of music. Play the first note D with RH 5. In the next measure, play the same note D but this time with the 4th finger. In the 3rd measure, play A with your 1st finger, and then in the last measure, play the same A with the 2nd finger. It's really very easy to do. The music of some pieces do not always lay out nicely for your fingers. This new technique will help to adjust your hand to be in a better position for the next note in certain musical passages. Play this line several times.

THE CAN-CAN

The Can-Can is a rousing piece written by a famous French composer, Jacques Offenbach. He wrote operas, operettas, ballets and chamber music. *The Can-Can* comes from his operetta, *Orpheus in the Underworld*. It's a very popular piece of music that I'm sure you've heard before.

When you start to learn this piece, notice not only the tempo and dynamic markings, but also the key signature. As you can see, there is a sharp sign on the F line, meaning all F's will be played F♯. The piece also begins and ends on G so it is in the key of G major.

Finger changes take place in the 4th and 6th measures. You can now see how useful finger changes on the same note can be to more easily perform the music that follows. In the second line, 3rd and 4th measures, there is a descending G major scale. Start softly than get gradually louder, as indicated by the *crescendo* marking, reaching a *forte* at the beginning of the third line. This makes for a pleasant change of dynamics and when done correctly, creates a dramatic reintroduction to the main theme.

The LH is made up entirely of G and D7 chords, both broken and blocked. Start your practice with the LH. It's easy and you'll then be able to concentrate more on your RH when you play them together. Begin by playing *forte* and at a bright speed.

When performing *The Can-Can,* imagine you're in a Parisian Bistro, enjoying the food, wine, music and dancers. You'll probably find you're enjoying performing this piece a little more. Music is, after all, a way of having fun. Imagining you're in other places while performing makes it even more fun.

A New Trick!

CHANGING FINGERS ON THE SAME NOTE: Sometimes it is necessary to replay the same note with a different finger. Practice the following line to prepare for *THE CAN-CAN.*

THE CAN-CAN

KEY OF G MAJOR
Key Signature: 1 sharp (F♯)

Jacques Offenbach

*Descending G major scale

The Primary Chords in G Major

Just as in the key of C major, the key of G major has its own three primary chords. On page 141, the top line of music shows the G major scale in the bass clef, but written an octave higher than where you originally played it on page 137. The 3 primary chords are once again built on the 1st, 4th and 5th notes of the scale and they are identified by the Roman numerals I, IV and V7.

Look down the left side of page 141 to the half music line, *Primary Chords in G.* Notice the key signature has a sharp on the 4th line F so all F's are played as F♯. The 3 chords from the top line of music have been rearranged so they can be played more smoothly in a chord progression. You have already learned these chords earlier in the book so the music won't be new to you.

The I or G chord is fingered 1-3-5, as you've played it before. To move to the IV or C chord, the 5th finger stays on G, raise the 3rd finger off B and place the 2nd finger on C, then move the 1st finger up to E.

To move from the IV chord to the V7 or D7 chord, the 5th finger moves down to F♯, the 2nd finger remains on C, and the 1st finger moves back down to D. Play these 3 primary chords in G several times, alternating by saying the names of the chord one time (G, C, D7) and their Roman numerals (I, IV, V7) the next.

The half music line to the right on page 141 is a *G Major Chord Progression* written out as a short exercise. Notice the key signature also has a sharp on the 4th line F so all F's are again played as F♯. Play this progression several times until you can play the chords one after the other very smoothly.

THE MARINES' HYMN

The Marines' Hymn will certainly be familiar to you, and it's also fun to play. Notice the red *Fine* under the first line at the end, and the red *D. C. al Fine* under the bottom line at the end. Just to remind you, when you complete the second line, go back to the beginning and play the first line again without missing a beat. While the end of the first line has a repeat sign, you only repeat it once, the first time you play the line.

The Marines' Hymn begins with an incomplete measure and the missing counts are found in the last measure of the first line. Notice that the second line also begins with an incomplete measure and its missing counts are found in the last measure of the second line. To create a *march* effect, play the 3 staccato chords at the end of each line very evenly and crisply. *The Marines' Hymn* is played *forte* throughout, as befits a march.

Notice the finger changes and movement that take place in the RH in the 1st and 2nd complete measures. When you start to play this march, I recommend you start with the LH alone (it contains only the 3 primary chords), then play the RH alone, before playing hands together.

The Primary Chords in G Major

Reviewing the G MAJOR SCALE, LH ascending

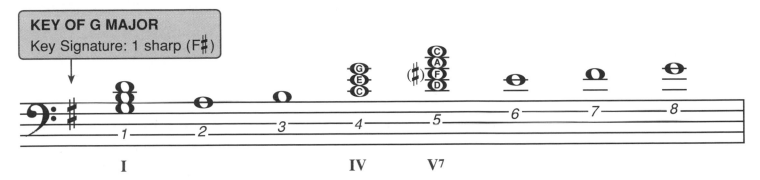

The following chord positions
(which you have already learned)
are used for smooth progressions:

Primary Chords in G

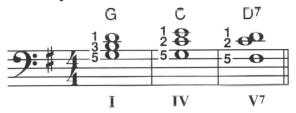

G Major Chord Progression with I, IV & V⁷ Chords

Play several times, saying the chord names
and numerals aloud:

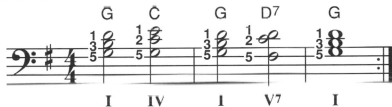

THE MARINES' HYMN 🔊48)))

Moderate march tempo

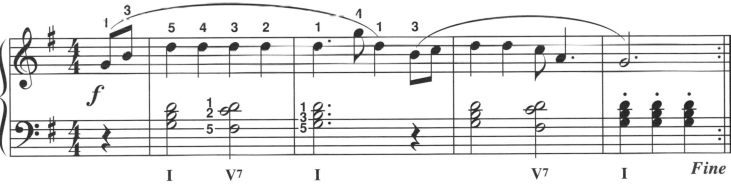

D. C. al Fine

Look at page 143, the page titled *Why Am I Blue?* There are several new items on the page: *syncopation*, the *natural sign*, and *1ˢᵗ and 2ⁿᵈ endings*.

The text at the top of the page defines *syncopated* notes. Basically, a *syncopated* note is played *between* the main beats of a measure (1-2-3-4) and held across the beat. In the upper right portion of the page, you will see a pattern with a *syncopated* note. The note played on the *&* count of 2 and held over the 3ʳᵈ count to the end of the measure is a *syncopated* note.

WHY AM I BLUE?

In the pink box, you are going to learn about a very important symbol. It is a *natural sign* and it cancels a sharp or a flat within a measure. Look at the last measure of the first line and you will see an F with a *natural sign*. Why the *natural sign*? Well, the key signature contains F♯, meaning all F's are to be played sharp. In this measure, however, the composer wants you to play an F natural.

There is another *natural sign* in the 1ˢᵗ measure of the third line to remind you that though B has been played flat in the two previous measures, in this measure the B is to be played natural—it's just a reminder. Sharps, flats and naturals not in the key signature are all called *accidentals*. When an *accidental* is used that is not really needed but used as a reminder, it is called a *courtesy accidental*.

One more thing, look at the last two measures of the piece. The next to the last measure has a 1 above the music, and the final measure has a 2 above the music. They are called 1ˢᵗ and 2ⁿᵈ endings and that pretty much describes what they mean. When you play *Why Am I Blue?* the first time and reach the 1ˢᵗ ending, you do not play the final measure but rather go back to the beginning and play the whole piece again. When you reach the 1ˢᵗ ending the second time, you skip it and go directly to the 2ⁿᵈ ending which ends the piece.

There are a few things to watch when you begin. We're in the key of G so every F is played sharp unless there is a natural sign in front of the note. The dynamic sign indicates the music is played moderately loud or *mezzo forte*. There are two *crescendo* signs and one *diminuendo* sign—see if you can find them. The LH consists of only the 3 primary chords in G. I'd recommend you start your practice playing the LH alone, then the RH alone, finally hands together. After you add the RH, make the song a little more interesting on the repeat by singing along with the lyrics. But don't feel too blue, it's only a song.

SYNCOPATED NOTE

Notes played between the main beats of the measure and held across the beat are called **SYNCOPATED NOTES.**

COUNT: 1 & 2 & 3 & 4 &

WHY AM I BLUE? 49 🔊))

> 🎵 The **NATURAL SIGN** cancels a sharp or flat!
> A note after a natural sign is always a *white key!*

Moderately slow blues tempo

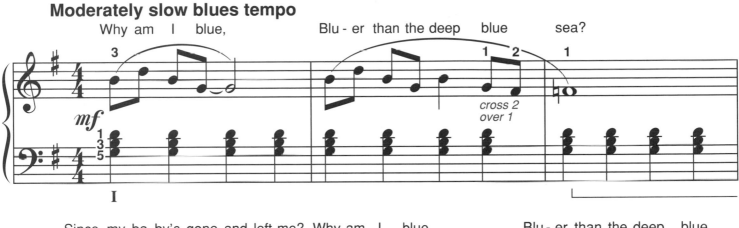

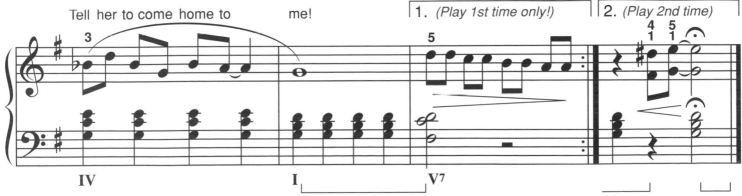

IMPORTANT!   Compare the Roman numerals in this piece with those in *GOT THOSE BLUES,* on page 131.

Now that you have mastered the keys of C and G major along with their scales and primary chords, you are going to move down a whole step from G to F for another scale, the F Major Scale on page 145.

The F Major Scale

When you learn each new scale and key, you will be using the same basic concept of starting with 2 tetrachords joined by a whole step. Look at the top music line and the first tetrachord beginning on F. From F, a whole step up is G, another whole step up is A, a half step up is, now this is a little tricky, not A♯ but B♭. Why not A♯? Because each note in a scale has to be in strict alphabetical order. If we said the first tetrachord is F-G-A-A♯, we would be repeating the letter A. To avoid the repetition and be musically correct, we lower the B a half step—same note, different name. So the first tetrachord is F-G-A-B♭.

Next we move up a whole step and start all over. Beginning on C we have a familiar tetrachord. Do you recognize it? If you said it is the first tetrachord in the C major scale, you would be correct—C, D, E and F.

Read the text under the top music line. It points out that the fingering of the F major scale for the LH is the same as for the C and G scales. Look at the first complete music line. The pink box at the beginning points to the key signature for the F major scale, a flat on the second line indicating that all B's are played as B♭. Play this scale several times and say the letter names as you play.

The next lower F scale on the page is in the treble clef. To play the F major scale with the RH requires a different fingering than for the other scales you've played. The first difference is the 5th finger is not used. The second difference is the fingering is 1-2-3-4, and then 1-2-3-4 again.

In the 1st measure of the scale, you can see that playing the B♭ with the 1st finger would be difficult. By playing the B♭ with the 4th finger and then passing the 1st finger under the 4th is much easier. It will be even easier if as soon as you play the 1st note F, you move your 1st finger to the base of the 3rd and 4th fingers and hold it there until it is needed. Keep your wrist even and move the hand smoothly along. Make certain you don't twist your wrist when the thumb moves under. Read the text above and below the RH scale before beginning to play—then play the F major scale several times, saying the finger numbers the first time and the letter names thereafter, until you become comfortable with this new fingering.

The next to the last line of music has the RH first playing the ascending F scale, then descending. The bottom line has the LH first playing the descending F scale, then ascending. This time I do not want you to play with your hands together in contrary motion as the fingering is not the same in each hand. When you play, always observe the repeat signs.

The F Major Scale

The fingering for the F MAJOR SCALE with the LH is the same as for all the scales you have studied so far: 5 4 3 2 1—3 2 1 ascending; 1 2 3—1 2 3 4 5 descending.

Play slowly and carefully!

To play the F MAJOR SCALE with the RH, the 5th finger is not used! The fingers fall in the following groups: 1 2 3 4—1 2 3 4 ascending; 4 3 2 1—4 3 2 1 descending.

Play slowly and carefully!

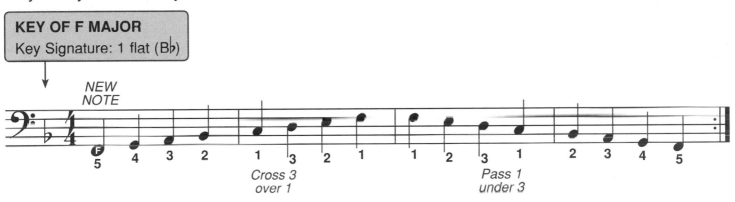

As soon as you play the thumb, move it under, carrying it at the base of the 3rd and 4th fingers until it is needed. Keep the wrist even, and move the hand smoothly along. Never twist the wrist when the thumb goes under.

Practice the F major scale several times daily. Begin slowly and gradually increase speed.

Play only with HANDS SEPARATE:

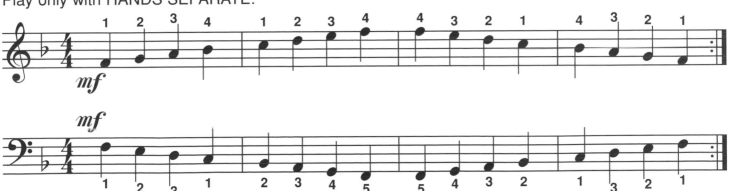

LITTLE BROWN JUG

Little Brown Jug on page 147 is another familiar folk song to add to your repertoire. New on this page is the *8th rest* and the *accent* sign. Look at the upper left pink box to see the 8th rest. It simply means you rest and do not play for the value of an 8th note. The only 8th rests in *Little Brown Jug* appear in the bass clef in the incomplete measure at the beginning of the piece, and then again at the end of the second line. At that point, after holding the previous notes for one and a half beats, you lift both hands off the piano as you count the "and" of the 4th beat.

The *accent sign* in the upper right pink box means to play the note under or over it with a special emphasis. You play the note somewhat louder than the previous note, but I don't want you to come down too hard on the keys. Accented notes still must sound musical. At the end of the first line of *Little Brown Jug*, there is an accent sign. There are more accent signs in the bottom two lines.

Little Brown Jug has a repeat sign in the bottom line, last measure, so the song is performed exactly the same the second time. It begins with an incomplete measure and the missing counts are found at the end of the second and fourth lines.

The dynamic signs are very important to performing *Little Brown Jug* properly. We start playing *mezzo forte* and as there is a long *crescendo* sign in the first line, we get gradually louder until we end the line with an accent. The second line is somewhat similar but without the accent sign at the end. The last 3 notes are played evenly. And of course, all the B's will be played as B♭. This is a happy song so have fun as you play.

147

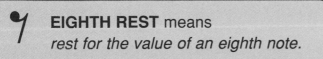

EIGHTH REST means
rest for the value of an eighth note.

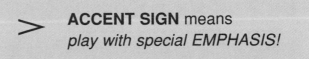

ACCENT SIGN means
play with special EMPHASIS!

LITTLE BROWN JUG

American folk song

The F Major Scale

1. Write the notes of the F MAJOR SCALE in the TREBLE staff under the squares.
   Use WHOLE NOTES.

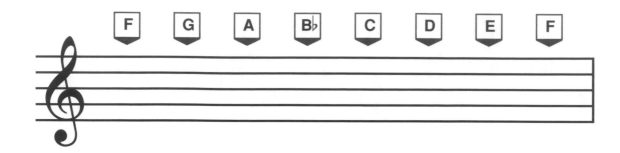

2. Write the notes of the F MAJOR SCALE in the BASS staff over the squares. Begin
   by writing the F under the bottom line of the staff. Use WHOLE NOTES.

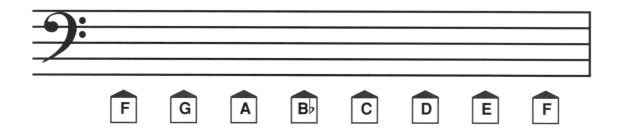

3. Write the name of each note in the square below it—then play and say the note names.

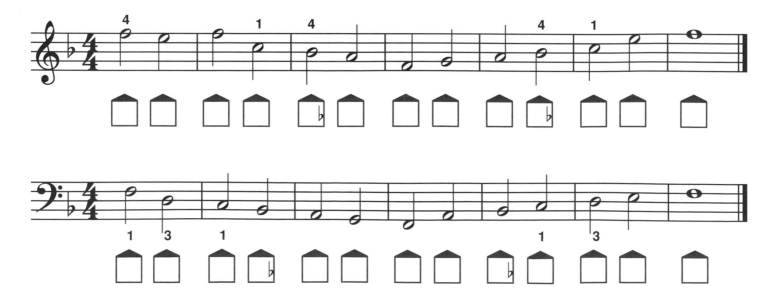

The Primary Chords in F Major

Knowing the F major scale prepares you to derive the 3 primary chords in F major. The 1st line of music below is the F major scale but written an octave higher than where you originally played it in the bass clef on page 145. The 3 primary chords are once again built on the 1st, 4th and 5th notes of the scale and they are identified by the Roman numerals I, IV and V7.

Look down the left side of this page to the half music line on the bottom of the page, *Primary Chords in F.* The 3 chords from the top line of music have been rearranged so they can be played more smoothly in a chord progression. Play the 3 chords several times, alternately saying "F, B♭, C7" the 1st time and "I chord, IV chord, and V7 chord" the next. Notice the key signature has a flat on the 2nd line so all B's are played as B♭.

The half music line to the right, *F Major Chord Progression with I, IV & V7 Chords* is an F major chord progression written out as a short exercise. Play this exercise several times, alternately saying "F, B♭, F, C7" the 1st time and "I chord, IV chord, I chord and V7 chord" the next. As these chords are all new to you, take a little extra time to become comfortable with the fingering.

The Primary Chords in F Major

Reviewing the F MAJOR SCALE, LH ascending

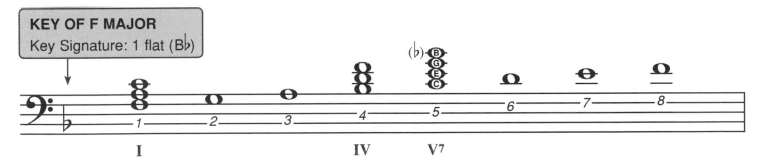

KEY OF F MAJOR
Key Signature: 1 flat (B♭)

The following chord positions are often used for smooth progressions:

Primary Chords in F

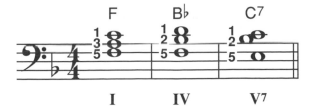

F Major Chord Progression with I, IV & V7 Chords

Play several times, saying the chord names and numerals aloud:

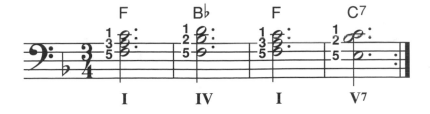

CHIAPANECAS
(MEXICAN HAND-CLAPPING SONG)

The chords and a different repeat sign are what is new in this rhythmic and rousing Mexican hand-clapping song titled *Chiapanecas*. On the bottom of page 151, read the explanation of the pair of repeat signs. Think of these repeat signs as bookends—all the music between them is repeated.

Next, look at the top of page 151 and you will see the first of the pair of repeat signs in the 1st measure under the red asterisk. Now look at the mirror image of that repeat sign at the end of the fourth line of music, also under the red asterisk. Everything between the pair of double bars is to be repeated. Normally, there will be no asterisks in the music.

I recommend you begin playing by studying the LH first. In the LH on this page, you are playing only F and C7 block chords. As the lettered chord symbols are written above the music, you will be able to recognize the chord by the music and the chord symbol. On page 151, the LH will be playing mostly broken chords. After the LH feels comfortable, begin playing the RH alone. In the 3rd measure on this page, you will be crossing your RH 2nd finger over your 1st. Finally, play both hands together.

First scan the music on both pages. We're in the key of F so all B's are played flat. We're also in $\frac{3}{4}$ time and we'll be playing moderately fast. When you have an audience, encourage them to clap the first 2 lines as you play. If your audience claps when you finish, you'll know you did a very good job.

CHIAPANECAS *(Mexican Hand-Clapping Song)*

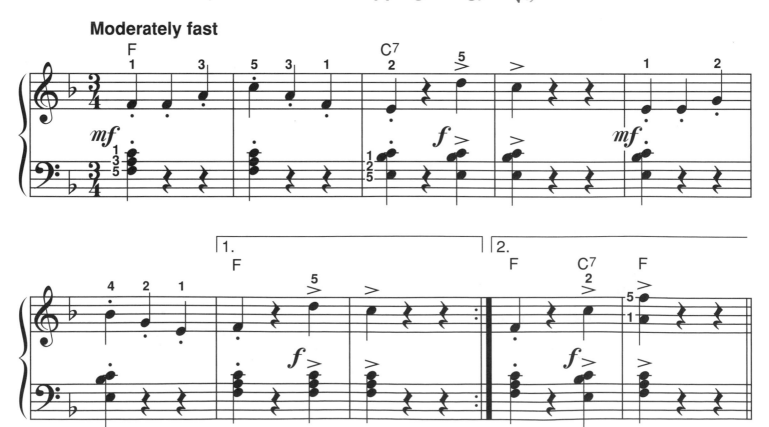

O SOLE MIO!

The rhythm of the bass part in *O Sole Mio!* will be new to you so we have included the counts under the 1st complete measure at the bottom of the page. Most of the music in the bass part of *O Sole Mio!* is simply broken F and C7 chords. Count and play the bass part of the first line of music until you feel secure with the rhythm.

It is all right to have a little fun when performing *O Sole Mio* by exaggerating the *fermatas* and the *ritardando*—the first line of music below and the last line on page 153. Notice that at the end of the 1st ending on page 153, you will be going back to the beginning of the piece on this page. The 2nd measure of the 2nd ending on page 153 has an *arpeggiated* chord on beat 3 which is played as a broken or rolled chord—read the explanation in the pink box below.

As always, scan the music first. The piece is in the key of F so all B's will be played as flats. The piece is played *forte* throughout except for a *diminuendo* in the 1st ending, and a *crescendo* and another *diminuendo* in the 2nd ending. All the block and broken chords are F and C7 chords with one exception. On page 153, second line, 3rd measure, and the 1st measure of the following line, there is a different chord. You have not learned this chord but you should be able to read the notes F-B♭-D♭ easily.

You can begin your preparation by playing the LH first, then playing the RH. In this piece, it would be effective to use a little more body movement than usual by swaying from side to side and back and forth as you feel the music. When you are fully prepared, play both hands together. When you can play *O Sole Mio* really well, play it for your family or some friends and then have a nice spaghetti dinner. It will be a wonderful evening, I promise you.

From Enrico Caruso to a recording entitled "In Concert," by José Carreras, Placido Domingo and Luciano Pavarotti, this great old favorite has provided tenors with wonderful encore material.

O SOLE MIO! 🔊 52

ARPEGGIATED CHORDS
When a wavy line appears beside a chord, the chord is *arpeggitated* (broken or rolled). Play the lowest note first, and quickly add the next highter notes one at a time until the chord is complete. The first note is played on the beat.

KEY OF F MAJOR
Key Signature: 1 flat (B♭)

Eduardo di Capua

Moderately slow

The Key of A Minor (Relative of C Major)

Read the text at the top of page 155 and you will learn that every major key has a relative minor key that has the same key signature. But the first or key note of the minor scale always starts on a different note than the major scale. The note it starts on is the 6th tone of the major scale.

Look for the heading *C Major Scale* that is printed in red a little down from the top of the page. See the C major scale below the heading? The 6th tone of the C major scale is A and that is where the A minor scale begins. Look below the major scale and you will see the *A minor scale*. The specific thing that makes the A minor scale a relative of the C major scale is they both have the same key signature. Neither C major nor A minor has any sharps or flats. Beginning the scale on A and playing the same 8 notes as the C major scale with no sharps and flats, gives you the A minor scale.

Play the C major scale first, which you already know. Then play the A minor scale right under it. Begin on A, and using the same fingering you used on the major scale, play the minor scale. Did you hear the difference? The name of this particular minor scale is the *Natural Minor Scale*. It is not called natural because it doesn't have any black keys, it is called natural because it simply follows the same sequence of notes as the major scale but starts on a different tone.

The A Harmonic Minor Scale

The natural minor scale is not the only minor scale. Look down the page for the title, *The A Harmonic Minor Scale*. The harmonic minor scale is the most frequently used minor scale. Look at the line of music under the pink box that is labeled *Key of A Minor*. It begins on the same note as the natural minor but in this case, the 7th tone is raised a half step. The 7th tone in the A natural minor scale is G and in the harmonic minor scale, that G becomes G♯. It gives the scale and the music played in that key a unique sound. Even though the music contains a G#, it is written as an accidental every time it appears and the key signature remains unchanged, in this case, no sharps or flats.

Starting with A, the lowest note of the scale, play and say the note names of the *A harmonic minor scale* with the RH ascending. When you reach the note F with your 3rd finger, stretch your 4th finger up to play the G♯. As you descend, after playing the G♯, stretch the 3rd finger down to F. It's an interesting sound, don't you think? Play the scale several times, listening carefully and becoming familiar with its sound.

Now play the A harmonic scale with the LH descending, the lowest line of music on the page. Starting with A, but this time the highest note of the scale, play and say the notes names of the scale. After you can play the A harmonic minor scale hands separately, you may play the hands together in contrary motion. When you play in contrary motion, the same numbered fingers on each hand play at the same time. Read through page 155 and play the A harmonic minor scale several times until you become familiar with the notes and the sound.

The Key of A Minor (Relative of C Major)

Every MAJOR key has a **RELATIVE MINOR** key that has the same KEY SIGNATURE.

The RELATIVE MINOR begins on the **6th** tone of the MAJOR scale.
The RELATIVE MINOR of C MAJOR is, therefore, A MINOR.

C MAJOR SCALE

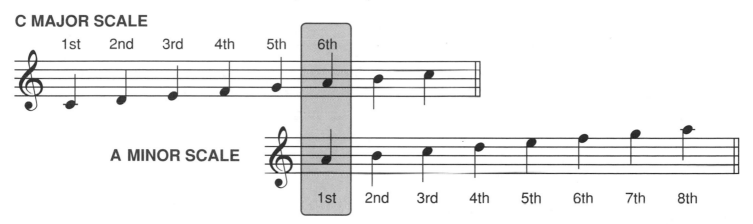

Because the keys of C MAJOR and A MINOR have the same KEY SIGNATURE (no sharps, no flats),
they are RELATIVES.

The minor scale shown above is called the **NATURAL MINOR SCALE.**
It uses only notes that are found in the relative major scale.

The A Harmonic Minor Scale

The most frequently used MINOR SCALE is the **HARMONIC MINOR.** In
this scale, the 7th tone is raised ascending and descending.

The raised 7th in the key of A MINOR is G♯. It is not included in the key
signature, but is written in as an "accidental" sharp each time it occurs.

Practice the A HARMONIC MINOR SCALE with hands separate. Begin slowly.

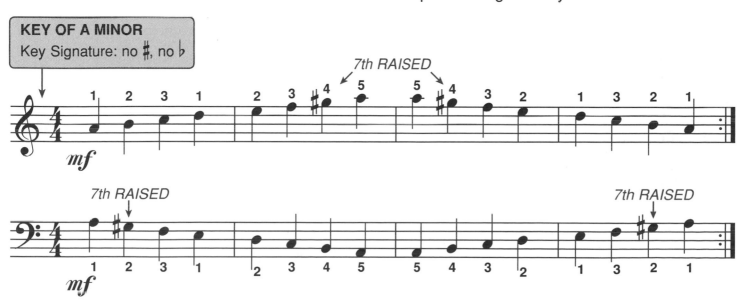

IMPORTANT! After you have learned the A HARMONIC MINOR SCALE with hands separate,
you may play the hands together in CONTRARY MOTION, by combining the
two staffs above.

More Syncopated Notes

At the top of page 157 in the pink box, you'll see the title, *More Syncopated Notes*. We first came across syncopated notes on page 143 in *Why Am I Blue?* Select any note with your RH and play and count the rhythm in the top line. It may feel a little odd at first but after a few attempts, I think you'll become an expert. Remember to hold the tied notes for their full value.

JERICHO

Jericho is a well-known spiritual that you've probably heard and possibly even sung. Look at the 2nd, 3rd and 4th measures of the first line of music. There are syncopated notes in each of the 3 measures. At the end of the second line, there is a 1st ending. When you play *Jericho* and complete the 1st ending, you will go back to the beginning and play the first line and a half again, then skip the 1st ending, and go directly to the 2nd ending.

I suggest starting your practice with the RH alone for the top 2 lines of music, adding the LH when you feel comfortable playing the syncopated notes.

The LH, beginning in the 2nd ending of the last line, will need a little more attention when you practice this piece. A good way to prepare this line when you reach it, is to first play the LH alone followed by hands together.

Jericho is played moderately fast, starting with the dynamic sign *mezzo forte*. The bottom line of music has a change of dynamics to *forte* along with many accent signs creating a dramatic ending. Holding the tied notes for their full value is the important thing to watch in *Jericho*.

Read the footnote at the bottom of the page explaining how to determine whether a piece is in a major key or its relative minor. As this piece has no sharps or flats in the key signature and as the last note of almost every piece ends on the key note of the scale, in this case A, *Jericho* is in the key of A minor.

MORE SYNCOPATED NOTES:

— SYNCOPATED NOTES —

COUNT: 1 & 2 & 3 & 4 &   1 & 2 & 3 & 4 &

JERICHO 53 🔊))

KEY OF A MINOR
Key Signature: no ♯, no ♭*

See how many syncopated notes you can find in *JERICHO*.

Moderately fast

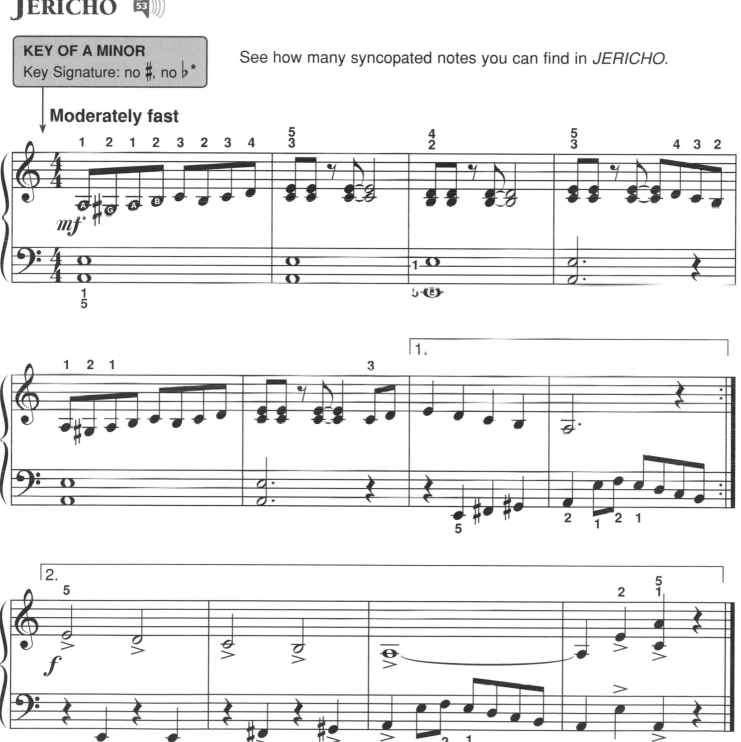

*To determine whether a piece is in a major key or its relative minor, look at the end of the piece. It will end on the key note or chord. This piece has no sharps or flats in the key signature and it ends on A (an A MINOR chord); therefore, the piece is in the key of A MINOR.

Reviewing the A Harmonic Minor Scale

1. Write the notes of the A HARMONIC MINOR SCALE in the TREBLE staff under the squares. Use WHOLE NOTES.

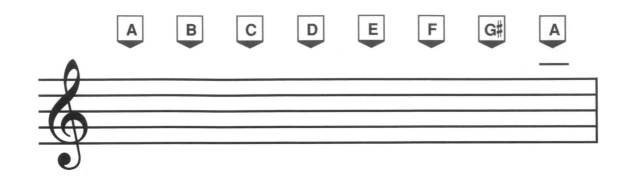

2. Write the notes of the A HARMONIC MINOR SCALE in the BASS staff over the squares. Use WHOLE NOTES.

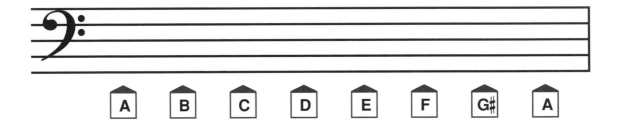

3. Write the name of each note in the square below it—then play and say the note names.

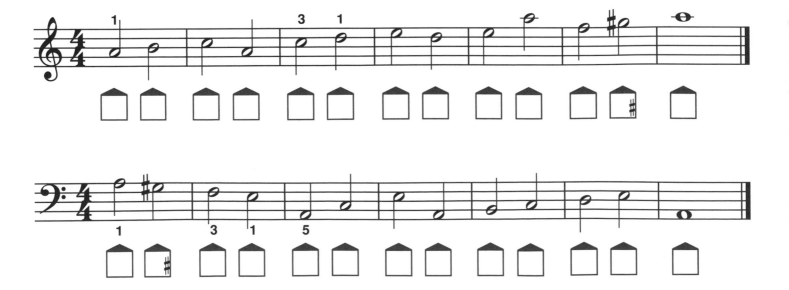

Introducing "Overlapping Pedal"

Though we have been using the pedal for a while, I am now going to introduce a new style that can make a dramatic difference in the way you sound. It is called *Overlapping Pedal* and you'll find it below on this page. Up until now, you have been using the pedal by pressing it down, holding it for a short while, and then releasing it. Now you will press the pedal down, lift it up, and immediately press it back down again.

The pedal's function is to lift the felt pads off the strings that are within the piano, allowing them to vibrate and continue to sound. To stop the sound, lift your right foot, allowing the pedal to rise. That allows the felt pads to come down onto the strings and stop the sound. Now you can play a new chord without any previously played notes being carried over.

Read the text on the lower half of this page and play the 2 lines of music, using the pedal as directed. Say *"up-down"* with the rise and fall of the pedal. The key to successful pedaling is that you do not pedal as you play a note or chord, but you pedal immediately after your fingers sound the notes. As the hand goes down, the foot comes up and quickly goes down again.

Introducing "Overlapping Pedal"

The following sign is used to indicate OVERLAPPING PEDAL.

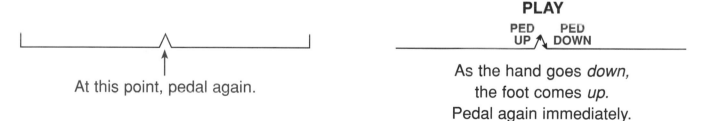

At this point, pedal again.

PLAY

PED   PED
UP   DOWN

As the hand goes *down,*
the foot comes *up.*
Pedal again immediately.

Practice the following exercises before playing *GREENSLEEVES.*

Self-Teaching Study Guide

GREENSLEEVES

You will be using a new dynamic sign in *Greensleeves*. It is *mp* which means to play *moderately soft*—a little louder than *piano* but not as loud as *mezzo-forte*. See the pink box to the right of the title *Greensleeves,* below.

To make fingering the music a little more comfortable, at times you will play a note with one finger, then while holding the note down, change to a different finger. On page 161, look at the third line of music, 3rd measure. The RH plays a half note D with the 1st finger, and while holding the note down, replaces the 1st finger with the 3rd finger. The same finger change happens again at the beginning of the bottom line, in the same situation.

Greensleeves is played at a moderately slow speed and *mezzo piano*. Because the piece is in A minor, many G's are played as sharps, so watch for them. There are also many F's played as sharped notes in *Greensleeves* so watch for them as well. After you have learned the piece, add the pedal. Make sure the music sounds are smoothly connected, not separated or blurry.

Take note of the *mf* at the beginning of the third line on page 161. Up until here, you have been playing *moderately soft*. Now you will be playing *moderately loud* until the end. It's a beautiful piece and I suspect you will enjoy playing *Greensleeves*. Begin your practice by first playing hands separately, then together.

GREENSLEEVES 🔊

NEW DYNAMIC SIGN

mp *(mezzo piano)* = medium soft

KEY OF A MINOR
Key Signature: no ♯, no ♭

*FINGER SUBSTITUTION: While holding the note down with 1, change to 3 on the 2nd beat.

More About Triads

Look at page 163, *More About Triads* and at red #1 just under the title, read the text. Some of the 3rds you have been playing are major 3rds and some have been minor 3rds. Think of a minor 3rd as being smaller than a major 3rd.

A *major 3rd* consists of 4 half steps. A *major 3rd* above C is E. A *minor 3rd* consists of 3 half steps. A *minor 3rd* above C is Eb. Any *major 3rd* can be changed to a minor *3rd* by lowering the upper note by one half step.

Look at red #2 and read the text. All the 5ths you have been playing so far have been *perfect 5ths*. A 5th consists of 7 half steps. A perfect 5th above C is G. As there are no major and minor 5ths in music, 5ths are called *perfect*.

Look at red #3 and read the text. As you know, a *major triad* is made up of 3 notes. It consists of a root, a major 3rd, and a perfect 5th. Look at red #4 to the right. A *minor triad* consists of a root, minor 3rd, and a perfect 5th. An easy way to construct a minor triad is to play a major triad and then lower the 3rd by a half step.

Look at red #5. The line of music below consists of a series of major triads followed by minor triads. Play this line several times, saying C major triad, C minor triad, etc. Then play this line an octave lower with the LH.

The Primary Chords in A Minor

The *Primary Chords in A Minor* are introduced on the bottom half of page 163. The line of music below the title reviews the ascending *A harmonic minor scale* (see page 155). The first triad on the staff is the *A minor chord*. To indicate minor triads and chords, we use small, lower case Roman numerals—you can see the lower case i under the Am chord. To the right, on the 4th note of the scale, is the D minor chord. The lower case iv is also under the chord. As with the major scales, the i and iv minor chords are built on the 1st and 4th notes of the scale.

The V chord, a major triad, is built on the 5th note of the scale and becomes a V7 chord by adding the 7th above the root of the chord—in this case, an E7 chord. The root of the V chord is E and the 7th above it is D. To play these chords in a smooth progression, the notes of the iv and V7 chords are rearranged. See the bottom left half line of music showing the 3 chords.

The i or A minor chord is fingered 5-3-1; the iv or D minor chord is fingered 5-2-1; the V7 or E7 chord is also fingered 5-2-1. See the bottom right half line of music showing the same 3 chords played an octave higher. Play the bottom lines several times, saying the Roman numerals the first time and the chord names on the repeat.

More About Triads

1. Some of the 3rds you have been playing are MAJOR 3rds, and some are MINOR (smaller) 3rds.

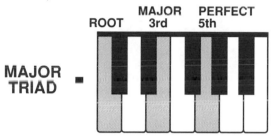

MAJOR 3rd (4 half steps) **MINOR 3rd** (3 half steps)

Any MAJOR 3rd may be changed to a MINOR 3rd by lowering the upper note one half step!

2. All of the 5ths you have played so far are PERFECT 5ths.

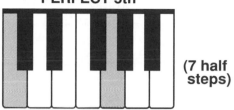

PERFECT 5th (7 half steps)

3. MAJOR TRIADS consist of a ROOT, MAJOR 3rd & PERFECT 5th.

MAJOR TRIAD =

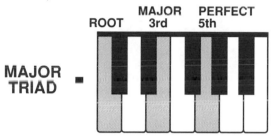

ROOT MAJOR 3rd PERFECT 5th

Any MAJOR triad may be changed to a MINOR triad by lowering the 3rd one half step!

4. MINOR TRIADS consist of a ROOT, MINOR 3rd & PERFECT 5th.

MINOR TRIAD =

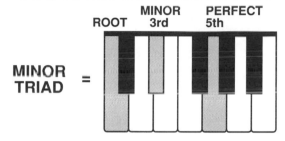

ROOT MINOR 3rd PERFECT 5th

5. Play the following triads with RH 1 3 5. Say "C major triad, C minor triad," etc., as you play each pair. Then repeat ONE OCTAVE LOWER, using LH 5 3 1.

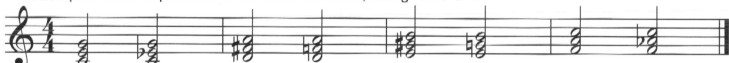

The Primary Chords in A Minor

Reviewing the A HARMONIC MINOR SCALE, LH ascending

Small (lower case) Roman numerals are used to indicate minor triads (**i** & **iv**).

Small (lower case) m = minor

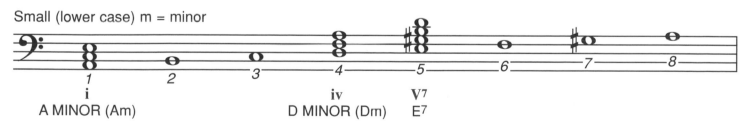

i — A MINOR (Am)   iv — D MINOR (Dm)   V7 — E7

The following positions are often used for smooth progressions:

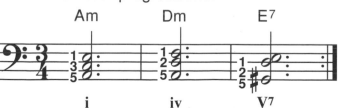

Am   Dm   E7

i   iv   V7

The same, one octave higher.

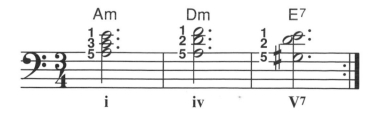

Am   Dm   E7

i   iv   V7

GO DOWN, MOSES

Go Down, Moses on page 165 is another familiar spiritual. If you can easily play the 3 primary chords in A minor, you will have little difficulty playing this spiritual.

I'd suggest you start by playing the LH alone and then adding the right. After you can comfortably play with hands together, add the pedal. The tempo is moderately slow and starts softly, *piano*. At the end of the first line, there is a *crescendo* sign leading up to playing *mezzo forte*. At the ending of the second line, there is a *diminuendo* sign leading back down to *piano*.

There is a dramatic change in the dynamics at the beginning of the third line, as if God is speaking to Moses. Play that line loud with accents in the first two measures. At the beginning of the bottom line, the dynamic sign is *mezzo forte*—play a little softer than *forte*. Then at the end of the bottom line, there is another *diminuendo* sign, ending softly, or *piano*. Because this spiritual is in the key of A harmonic minor, all G's will be played as G♯ and have an accidental sharp sign in front of the note.

For a really effective rendition of *Go Down, Moses*, the proper use of the pedal is essential. Because you will be mixing 3-note chords in the LH with a melody note in the RH, the use of the pedal will make those notes resonate and add an intensity to the music not attainable without the pedal.

Finally, add your own voice to the music by singing the song. When you sing, follow the dynamic signs in the same manner as when you play the notes.

GO DOWN, MOSES

The Key of D Minor (Relative of F Major)

You have played in the key of A minor, which is the relative minor of C major. We are now going to move on to another minor key on page 167, the key of D minor, which is the relative minor of F major.

Look down the page to the *F Major Scale*. As you remember from the key of A minor, the minor scale begins on the 6th tone of its relative major. As the 6th tone of the F major scale is D, the relative minor scale begins on D. Now, starting on D but using the same key signature of F major (B♭), play the D minor scale just to hear what it sounds like. That is the D natural minor scale, but you will mostly be playing the D harmonic minor scale. Read through the top half of page 167 and play the F major scale followed by the D minor scale. Remember that all the B's are played flat.

The D Harmonic Minor Scale

Look half way down page 167 to the title *The D Harmonic Minor Scale*. Read the text below the title. In the harmonic minor scale, the 7th tone is raised when playing ascending and descending. The raised 7th in D minor is C♯ but it is not included in the key signature—an accidental sharp is placed before every C that appears in the music.

Now look at the first complete line of music near the bottom of the page. It is the ascending D harmonic minor scale for the RH. There is a B♭ in the key signature and an accidental C♯ in the music. Play the D harmonic minor scale several times, saying B♭ and C♯ every time those notes appear in the scale.

The bottom line of music is the descending D harmonic minor scale for the LH. Once again, there is a B♭ in the key signature and an accidental C♯ in the music. Play the D harmonic minor scale several times, saying B♭ and C♯ every time those notes appear. After you have learned this scale with hands separate, play with hands together in contrary motion.

The Key of D Minor (Relative of F Major)

D MINOR is the relative of **F MAJOR**.
Both keys have the same key signature (1 flat, B♭).

REMEMBER: The RELATIVE MINOR begins on the **6th** tone of the major scale.
The relative minor of F MAJOR is, therefore, D MINOR.

F MAJOR SCALE

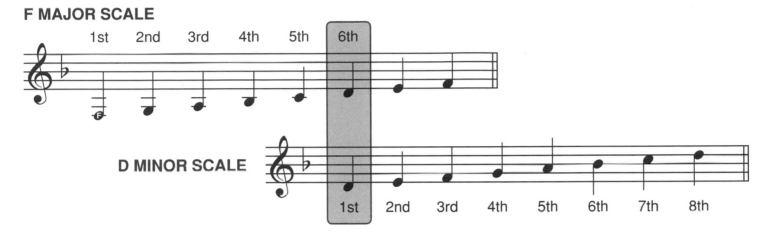

The minor scale shown above is the NATURAL MINOR scale. Remember, the natural minor uses only notes that are found in the relative major scale.

The D Harmonic Minor Scale

In the HARMONIC MINOR scale, the 7th tone is raised ascending and descending.

The raised 7th in the key of D MINOR is C♯. It is not included in the key signature, but is written as an "accidental" sharp each time it occurs.

Practice the D HARMONIC MINOR scale with hands separate. Begin slowly.

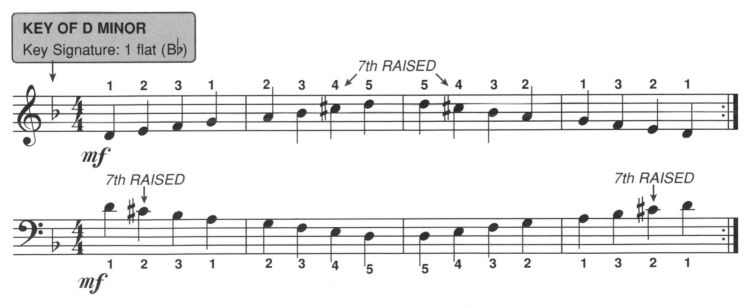

IMPORTANT! After you have learned the D HARMONIC MINOR SCALE with hands separate, you may play the hands together in CONTRARY MOTION, by combining the two staffs above.

SCARBOROUGH FAIR

Scarborough Fair is a beautiful melody and is on page 169. The pink box on the upper right part of the page highlights a new dynamic sign, *pp* *(pianissimo)* and indicates you are to play very softly, even softer than *piano*.

A quick scan of the music reveals the song is played moderately slow, is in 3/4 time, and has a key signature of one flat, B♭. Notice also that in *Scarborough Fair*, the LH plays only broken chords throughout. At the time *Scarborough Fair* first became popular a long time ago, its accompaniment part might have been played on a *lute*, an old stringed instrument, using broken chords. There is a repeat sign just before the last 2 measures at the bottom of the page that takes you back to the 3rd measure on the top line of music. On the repeat, the RH plays an octave higher. Those instructions are written above the lyric of the 3rd measure.

I hope you enjoy performing *Scarborough Fair*, a haunting song with a minor sound that tells the sad story of an old romance whose flame appears to not have been completely extinguished. Do you think you can start to learn *Scarborough Fair* by playing both hands together? Learn the notes first, and then add the changing dynamic signs, the *crescendo* and *diminuendo* signs and, very importantly, the pedal. Remember to end very softly as you also slow down in the last two measures.

SCARBOROUGH FAIR

NEW DYNAMIC SIGN

pp (*pianissimo*) = very soft

KEY OF D MINOR
Key Signature: 1 flat (B♭)

The Primary Chords in D Minor

After learning the key of D harmonic minor the next step, just as with the A minor scale, is to learn the 3 primary chords. Look at the bottom half of this page titled *The Primary Chords in D Minor*. The 3 primary chords are derived the same way that all primary chords are formed.

The first complete line of music below is the *D harmonic minor scale*. The key signature is one flat, B♭, same as the relative F major scale, but it will also include an accidental C♯ in the music. Next, learn to play the lower two half lines of music which are the chords rearranged for smooth progressions.

When you complete this page, turn to page 172 to play *Raisins and Almonds,* a beautiful old folk song of childhood memories.

The Primary Chords in D Minor

Reviewing the D HARMONIC MINOR SCALE, LH ascending

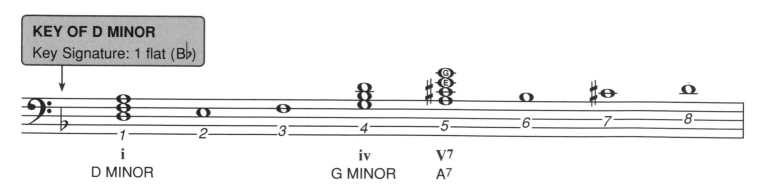

KEY OF D MINOR
Key Signature: 1 flat (B♭)

i — D MINOR   iv — G MINOR   V⁷ — A⁷

The following positions are often used for smooth progressions:

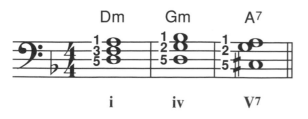

Dm   Gm   A⁷

i   iv   V⁷

Play several times, saying the chord names and numerals aloud:

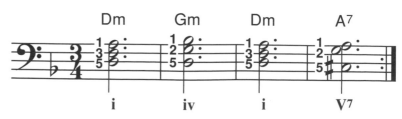

Dm   Gm   Dm   A⁷

i   iv   i   V⁷

STUDY GUIDE FOR PAGES 174–175

We've been together for a long while and you are rapidly nearing the end of this book. As a writer, it is a little sad for me because I've enjoyed describing the joys of playing the piano along with the basic concepts of music. In another way, I'm pleased that you are still progressing and learning more about music and the piano. You've only got a little way to go now and I've saved the best for last. The book ends with five very special piano arrangements, all of them suitable for performance at any gathering you have scheduled in the near future.

HE'S GOT THE WHOLE WORLD IN HIS HANDS

The arrangement of *He's Got the Whole World in His Hands* is on pages 174 and 175. Here is a spiritual that is uniquely arranged—within one piece you will be playing in 3 different keys. As you already know the I, IV and V7 chords in the keys of C, G and F major, *He's Got the Whole World in His Hands* will be a very good review for you. Before you begin to play, take some time to review and play the primary chords in C major (page 129), in G major (page 141), and in F major (page 149). This will be a good preparation and review for you.

There is some *syncopation* in the piece so before you begin, play and count the RH of the top three lines on page 174, which is in the key of G major, to prepare you to properly play the syncopated notes. The music is almost the same in all 3 keys so if you can play the first section with your RH, you should have no trouble playing the other two.

Notice that the dynamic signs change for each key. Also note the *ritardando* three measures from the end on page 175 as the spiritual slowly comes to an end. There is also some pedaling in the last two measures to create an appropriate ending.

I would suggest you learn both hands separately before playing hands together.

RAISINS AND ALMONDS

The folk song *Raisins and Almonds* on the bottom of this page consists almost entirely of broken chords for the LH, so you will have to be able to play these chords easily and smoothly before beginning. *Raisins and Almonds* is in the key of D harmonic minor. That means there is a B♭ in the key signature and all C's have an accidental sharp. Scan the music on your own, making note of the tempo, the changing dynamics, the *crescendo* and *diminuendo* signs, and the pedaling. Learn the LH thoroughly before adding the RH as coordinating the two hands here is a little more complicated. When you can easily play *Raisins and Almonds*, a folk song reflecting upon early childhood memories, sing along with the lyrics.

The next lower line of music is the D harmonic minor progression with broken i, iv and V7 chords. Play this exercise several times. This will be very beneficial to you when you learn to play *Raisins and Almonds*.

D MINOR PROGRESSION with broken i, iv & V⁷ chords

Play several times.

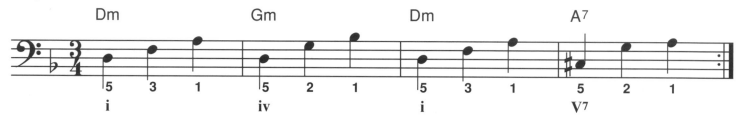

RAISINS AND ALMONDS 🔊

Folk song

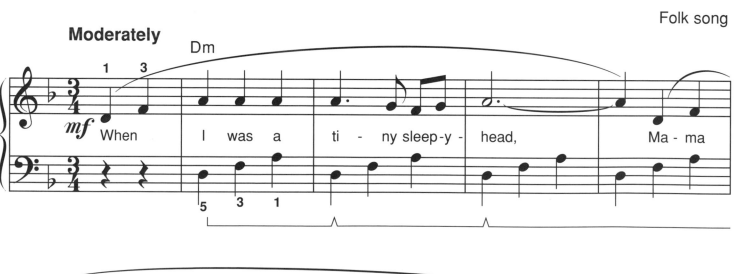

HE'S GOT THE WHOLE WORLD IN HIS HANDS

This piece reviews the **I, IV & V⁷** chords of the keys of G MAJOR, C MAJOR and F MAJOR.
It also reviews syncopated notes, in preparation for *THE ENTERTAINER,* on pages 178–179.

KEY OF G MAJOR
Key Signature: 1 sharp (F♯)

Moderately & rhythmically

KEY OF C MAJOR
Key Signature: no ♯, no ♭

KEY OF F MAJOR
Key Signature: 1 flat (B♭)

ritardando

(A - men!)

LH Warm-Up

Before you begin, practice the 4 measure exercise for the LH at the top of page 178, *LH Warm-Up*. Make sure you can play this line smoothly and steadily before moving on to *The Entertainer*.

The Entertainer is one of my favorites and I think you will enjoy it, too. The piece contains a lot of syncopated notes for the RH, in fact there is at least one in almost every measure. If you were not confident in your playing of syncopated notes before, you will be an expert by the time you finish this piece.

THE ENTERTAINER

Scott Joplin was a popular composer in the early 1900s and was well-known for his ragtime compositions. Ragtime was a popular musical form at the turn of the 20th century and it strongly influenced early jazz musicians. Joplin's music and ragtime had a revival in the early 1970s when the award-winning film *The Sting* was released.

Scan the music for *The Entertainer*. There is a 1st and 2nd ending at the end of piece on page 179. When you are playing and reach the end of the 1st ending, go back to the beginning of the bottom line on page 178, where you will see the first of the paired repeat signs.

When you perform this piece, take extra care to play the 8th notes evenly—that's one of the trademarks of *ragtime*. Later, when *swing* became popular, the 8th notes were played unevenly. The very last note in the 2nd ending on page 179 is a bass C which you haven't played before. It's easy to find as it is a 5th down from G, which you do know.

Before you begin practicing *The Entertainer*, I would like you to play and count the RH for 3 of the most complicated rhythms. The tempo of the music, and these are Joplin's words, is "Not fast!"

1. Play the RH and count the first 3 measures on page 178.

2. Starting with the last pair of 8th notes on the second line on page 178, play until the 3rd beat of the 1st measure on page 179.

3. Starting with the last pair of 8th notes on the top line of page 179, play until the third beat of the 2nd measure, second line.

If you can play these measures at a steady, even tempo, you will be well on your way to being able to play *The Entertainer,* hands together, without too much difficulty. I would highly recommend you start your practice by learning the entire RH first. Take it in small segments like I just did. *The Entertainer* is certainly a fun piece to play. You've now come a long way in your ability to play the piano.

Eighth Note Triplets

Eighth Note Triplets are introduced at the top of page 180. Read through the explanation. Triplets are played 3 notes to one beat. When 3 notes are grouped together with a figure 3 above or below the notes, the group is called a *triplet*. The 3 notes of an 8th note triplet equal one quarter note. Triplets can be counted in a number of ways: "trip-a-let" or "one-&-then" or any way that will convey to you the grouping of 3 notes on 1 beat.

AMAZING GRACE

Also new on this page is the word *simile*, seen in the last measure of the first line of *Amazing Grace*. The footnote describes *simile* as "continue playing in the same manner." In this case, the triplets will not have a 3 over or under the notes but you are expected to play them all as triplets.

I'd like you to play the RH alone when you start playing *Amazing Grace*, counting the triplets as you play. After that, practice the LH alone. There are only 3 measures in the LH that include triplets and 2 of them are the same. One is in the last measure of the second line on page 180. The same measure appears on page 181 at the end of the third line. The last triplet is in the next-to-last measure of the piece. When you practice the LH, be sure to include the pedal as you play. After you can play hands separately well, only then play *Amazing Grace* with hands together.

The tempo of *Amazing Grace* is moderately slow and you start by playing *piano* and *legato with feeling*. The pedal is important to attain a legato and smoothly connected sound. Look down to the third line, 1st measure, on page 180. There is a very important *crescendo* in the measure. Continue to play a little louder, probably at *mezzo piano*, until you reach the 1st beat of the 4th measure of the first line on page 181. Now play *diminuendo* until you are back down to *piano*.

The second line of music on page 181 has a dramatic change in volume to *mezzo forte* and continues that way until the bottom line. The repeated ending is played *piano* the first time with a *diminuendo* in the last two measures, leading to a *pianissimo* the second time. The last two measures are played even softer, with the RH playing an octave lower on the repeat. The effectiveness of your performance depends mostly on your observing these changes in dynamics very carefully.

I particularly like playing the *arpeggiated* chords, or rolled chords, on page 181—they were first introduced on page 153. You play the lowest note first and quickly add the next higher notes one at a time.

This brings us to the end of our lessons in *Alfred's Self-Teaching Adult Piano Course*. I hope these lessons have been as much fun for you as they have been for me in presenting them to you. I hope you will continue playing and enjoying the piano for many, many more years.

LH Warm-Up

Practice many times, very slowly. These four measures contain everything new that you will find in the LH of *THE ENTERTAINER!*

THE ENTERTAINER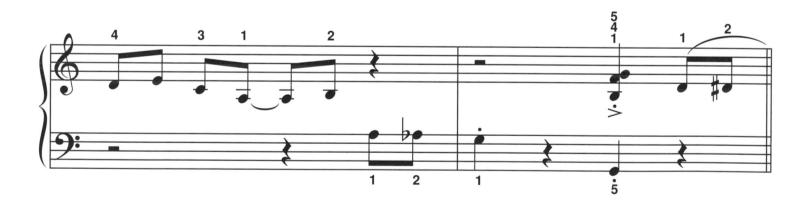

Scott Joplin

Not fast!*

* "Not fast" is the composer's own indication!

Eighth Note Triplets

When three notes are grouped together with a figure "*3*" above or below the notes, the group is called a **TRIPLET**.

The three notes of an eighth-note triplet group = one quarter note.

When a piece contains triplets, count **"trip-a-let"**

or **"one & then"**

or any way suggested by your teacher.

AMAZING GRACE

John Newton, J. Carrell & D. Clayton

Moderately slow

* simile = same. This means *continue playing in the same manner.* In this case, continue to play triplets each time three eighth notes are joined with one beam.

On pages 182 to 191 are five very popular selections that you have the knowledge and ability to perform. There are no *Study Guides* for these pages as they contain nothing new.

OVER THE RAINBOW

Music by HAROLD ARLEN
Lyrics by E.Y. HARBURG

At Last

Music by HARRY WARREN
Lyric by MACK GORDON

Slowly, with feeling

* The eighth notes may be played a bit unevenly: long short long short, *etc.*

Singin' in the Rain

Music by NACIO HERB BROWN
Lyric by ARTHUR FREED

* The eighth notes may be played a bit unevenly:

long   short   long   short, *etc.*

Laura

Lyrics by JOHNNY MERCER
Music by DAVID RAKSIN

Slowly, with expression

Have Yourself a
Merry Little Christmas

Words and Music by HUGH
MARTIN and RALPH BLANE

Epilogue

You might be wondering, "What happens now?"

As you really know a lot, you have the capability of performing quite a bit of your favorite music, from popular hits of Broadway and motion pictures, to classical and sacred music, to old standards, even popular music of today. Look for your favorite kind of music by browsing in your local music store or on the website of an internet music store.

Another choice you have is to continue your lessons. *Alfred's Basic Adult Course* continues on to Book 2 (#2461—Book only) **or** (#18105—Book & CD) and Book 3 (#2263). There is also a more expanded version of these books, *Alfred's Basic Adult All-in-One Course*, Book 2 (#14514) and Book 3 (#14534). As this course is very popular, you can probably find them in any music store.

Now that you have progressed this far, and if you haven't already, you might also want to consider finding a local piano teacher to help you progress further. A professional teacher is always preferred over self-study. A teacher will correct mistakes quickly and be able to demonstrate the proper way to play a piece or musical passage. A teacher can also recommend other music books for your grade level to widen your repertoire. Look for more Alfred books at our website, Alfred.com.

But more than that, with your ability to play the piano, a whole new world of music is now open to you. There are probably a number of places near you where a pianist is performing. It can be at a concert hall where classical music is being played, or it can be at a restaurant or cocktail lounge where a local pianist is performing popular standards.

By watching many pianists of varying skills, you can learn even more. Notice the way they use their body to enhance the style of music they are playing. Watch as a pianist performs a Debussy impressionistic piece like *Clair de lune,* or see another pianist as he/she plays a jazz version of *Fascinatin' Rhythm.* Their posture and intensity will be guided by the style of the music. There is much to learn by observing.

I always like to watch a pianist's hands as they play, especially if I am familiar with the music. Each musician tends to interpret music in their own unique way, and it is those differences that will give you new insight into the music. I think you will find there is now so much more to enjoy with music as you listen actively, rather than passively—and it all began when you started to learn how to play the piano.

I promised you at the beginning of the book that music will make your life more interesting and exciting once you learn how to play the piano. I hope you feel I've kept my promise.